The Children Act Guidance and Regulations

Volume 2
Family Support, Day Care and Educational Provision for Young Children

A NEW FRAMEWORK FOR THE CARE AND UPBRINGING OF CHILDREN

LONDON: HMSO

© Crown copyright 1991
First published 1991
Third impression 1991
ISBN 0 11 321372 7

Preface

This volume contains guidance on Part III (Local Authority Support for Children and their Families) and Part X (Child Minding and Day Care for Young Children) of the Children Act 1989 (referred to as the Act throughout). It is issued under section 7 of the Local Authority Social Services Act 1970 which requires local authorities in the exercise of their social services functions to act under the general guidance of the Secretary of State.

Throughout the document the phrase 'local authorities' is used. It should be noted that under the provisions of the 1970 Act certain functions are referred to the Social Services Committee of a local authority and, unless otherwise stated, references to a local authority in this document denotes the Social Services Committee and its officers. Certain sections of the document are, however, explicitly addressed to local education authorities. This document treats the Act as if it were in force now and uses the past tense to refer to the legislation which is repealed by the Act.

Chapters 1 to 3 contain guidance on local authority responsibilities for children in need and their families. Chapters 4 to 9 deal with services used by young children – under fives attending day care or educational provision and children up to the age of 8 attending out- of-school or holiday schemes. The principal points of concern to local education authorities are contained in chapters 6, 7 and 9.

This guidance supersedes Ministry of Health circulars 5/65, 36/68 and 37/68 and Department of Health Circular LASS(76)3, Department of Education and Science Circular 2/73, and the following joint Department of Health/Department of Education and Science letters:

DH ref: LASSL(76)5

DES ref: S.21/47/05
(issued on 9 March 1976)

DH ref: LASSL(78)1, HN(78)5

DES ref: S.47/24/013
(issued on 25 January 1978)

Contents

CHAPTER 1   INTRODUCTION

1.1. The guidance is intended to provide a clear statement of the requirements placed on local authorities by the Children Act 1989. This is to help local authorities develop effective strategies and policies and provide practitioners with a robust framework within which to work. This volume aims to identify changes and explain the underlying principles in relation to family support services for families with children in need and day care services for young children. It discusses the implications for policies, procedures and practice. In addition it considers day care services for under fives and educational provision for that age group together because of the particular need for close co-operation in respect of services for under fives.

1.2. The Act brings together most private and public law about children, thereby replacing complex and fragmented legislation with a single statute. Part III together with Schedule 2 sets out the main responsibilities of local authorities for children in their area who are in need and their families and for children in need whom they look after. It also draws together local authorities' functions towards children which existed under the Child Care Act 1980, the National Assistance Act 1948 and Schedule 8 of the National Health Service Act 1977 in relation to children with disabilities and under fives. All these provisions reflect the Act's philosophy that the best place for the child to be brought up is usually in his own family and that the child in need (who includes the child with disabilities) can be helped most effectively if the local authority, working in partnership with the parents, provides a range and level of services appropriate to the child's needs. To this end the parents and the child (where he is of sufficient understanding) need to be given the opportunity to make their wishes and feelings known and to participate in decision-making.

1.3. Part III gives local authorities a range of new duties, including identification of children who are in need, support of children's links with their families, provision of day care and setting up of procedures to consider representations about the provision of services. Under Part III children with disabilities are treated first as children and then as persons with a disability. They therefore benefit from safeguards which were unavailable to them under previous legislation unless they were in the care of a local authority. The local authorities' general welfare duty under section 22(3) and their duty to review plans for children provide an additional safeguard to such children's welfare.

1.4. This statement of existing responsibilities with new and important improvements should help to focus attention on the role of local authorities in supporting the family in various ways. In considering the provisions of the Act and the implications for policies and practice it is important to bear in mind the concept of parental responsibility set out in Part I of the Act. Part I contains provisions about the means of acquisition of parental responsibility, when it may be exercised and the effect of orders made under the Act. Parental responsibility is conceived as encompassing both the obligations and the corresponding rights of parents which flow from their responsibility. The Act provides that parental responsibility is not affected by parental separation or divorce. Even where courts intervene in the family's life the duty on both parents to contribute to their child's upbringing remains. Annex A reproduces the explanation of parental responsibility in **An Introduction to the Children Act 1989** (HMSO December 1989) and provides a note on private law proceedings.

1.5. Within this volume the provision of foster placements and residential accommodation is discussed in the context of the general principles of service provision. Regulations and guidance on planning, review, representations, foster placements and residential placements are in separate volumes in this series. Child protection issues are referred to within this document but readers will need to refer to volume 1 and **Working Together** for detailed guidance. This volume should be read in conjunction with the other volumes in this series and the **Principles and Practice in Regulations and Guidance**.

1.6. Part III also introduces the review duty under which local authorities working with local education authorities are required to review and report on the day care services in their area used by children aged under 8. This new duty, the general duty to provide day care for children inn need (Section 18) and the modernised registration system in Part X of the Act to regulate independent day care services and childminding used by children aged under 8 give local authorities for the first time a clear function to oversee and co-ordinate these services. This is expected to result in more efficient use of existing services and coherent development of new ones, and in particular to take full account of the potential of the private and voluntary sectors.

1.7. Attached to this guidance is a short bibliography of publications on family support, day care services and early years education and a list of codes of practice prepared by various national voluntary organisations for different day care services used by young children. This is intended to provide policy workers, practitioners and service providers with a basic reading list as at the time of publication.

1.8. The Act requires a corporate local authority policy on implementation that will cover all the issues including those which require collaboration and corporate planning. Although responsibility for implementation rests mainly with the Social Services Committee and its officers, the Act is directed at the local authority as a whole and cannot succeed without effective inter-departmental collaboration at all levels. The local authority as a whole should therefore have an agreed and approved policy on family support services for children and their families and day care and educational provision for children under statutory school age. Steps should be taken to ensure that such a policy is developed and agreed, involving all relevant departments and organisations in the process. It should include arrangements for monitoring and implementation.

Policy Issues

1.9 Local authorities will need to review all their existing child care policies, their priorities will need to be re-examined and rethought in the light of the Children Act. Priorities in resource allocation must be identified and related to budgeting strategies; there will be a need to re-evaluate service delivery in liaison with the voluntary and private sector and to work out an information strategy. Paragraph 1(1) of Schedule 2 requires that local authorities take reasonable steps to identify the extent to which there are children in need in their area. Under the provisions of the Act children with disabilities should be given the opportunity to lead lives which are as normal as possible. Therefore services for children with disabilities should be integrated with those provided for other children in need. Part III brings together the two streams of law covering local authority responsibilities to families with children: previous childcare legislation and the health and welfare statutes dealing mainly with children and disabilities. The intention is that local authorities should integrate service provision for all children who are in need, for whatever reason. In order to plan service provision, local authorities should integrate service provision for all children who are in need, for whatever reason. In order to plan service provision, local authorities will have to adapt existing information gathering systems so as to identify the need for services in their area and gaps in provision.

1.10. The Act's emphasis on family support and partnership with parents requires local authorities to adopt a new approach to child care services. To give family support a high priority in resource allocation may require new thinking across departments on matters such as devolving budget management and accountability.

1.11. The messages of research are important for local authorities in developing their child care policies. A companion volume in this series **Patterns and Outcomes in Child Placements** contains a current evaluation of those messages and should be read in conjunction with this volume of guidance.

Welfare Responsibilities

1.12 One of the key principles underpinning the Act is that local authorities must act to protect children from the harm which arises from family breakdown or abuse within the family, but avoid unwarranted intervention in families' lives or unnecessary weakening of family ties. Their responsibilities to promote and safeguard the welfare of children apply to children in local authority care and those being provided with accommodation under voluntary arrangements. That is to say they cover all children looked after by a local authority. In carrying out these responsibilities local authorities must have regard to these key requirements: due consideration to be given to the wishes and feelings of the child, parents, any other person with parental responsibility for the child and persons whose views the local authority consider relevant; due consideration to be given to the child's religious persuasion, racial origin and cultural and linguistic background.

Co-ordination, Collaboration and Co-operation

1.13 The Act puts the responsibility firmly on local authorities to provide accommodation, advice and assistance for children and young people in certain circumstances where such measures are needed to safeguard and promote their welfare. This may involve a social services department of a local authority requesting help from a local housing authority which, under section 27 of the Act, shall comply with a request for help if it is compatible with their statutory functions and does not unduly prejudice the discharge of those functions. Under the same provision the department will on occasion turn to the education authority for assistance in meeting the duties placed on the social services department in respect of family support. Sections 17(5), 27, 28 and 30 provide duties and powers in relation to co-operation between and consultation with different authorities including social services, education departments and housing authorities, health authorities and independent organisations. In relation to a child who has special educational needs, the social services department is under a duty (section 27(4)) to help the education department in the provision of services, and to consult the education department maintaining a child's statement of special educational needs (made under the Education Act 1981) when placing a child at an establishment providing education (section 28(1)). A corporate policy and clear departmental procedures in respect of interdepartmental collaboration will ensure good co-operation at all levels.

1.14. The local authority carries the principal responsibility for co-ordinating and providing services for children in need. In some cases their services will be supportive of other key agencies. The local authority and other relevant agencies remain responsible for decisions about their own service provision or legal and administrative issues assigned to them. They should, however, seek out and have available the best relevant help from other agencies. Similarly they must be available and prepared to contribute to the work of other key agencies in meeting the legitimate needs of children and their families. New organisational links between local authorities and health authorities will be needed in order to implement the Act fully in relation to chronically sick and disabled children and their parents.

1.15. Policies on community care under the NHS and Community Care Act 1990 and service provision under the Children Act should be considered together in respect of the requirement in each case to assess need and deliver services in accordance with available resources. The more formalised approach in community care to assessment, planning and delivery of services and the greater emphasis on the statutory protective element in children's services may require different relationships with other agencies and different styles of working. However, the essential functions are not different in principle and should not lead to operational difficulties if all concerned have a clear understanding of the approach required in the respective areas of work.

1.16. In the case of day care and education services for young children the importance of co-ordination between different local authority departments – particularly but not exclusively social services and education – has long been recognised. A co-ordinated approach is a means of ensuring that all children, whatever type of service they attend, have access to a good quality curriculum or programme with continuity of experience and smooth transition to other forms of day care or education. There are three levels at which co-ordination is needed: policy making, day-to-day operation of services and between staff working on different settings. A co-ordinated approach helps to create an environment where people with different qualifications and experience can share skills and expertise and ideas in a positive way. It is important for all departments within a local authority to find ways of encouraging staff to work with this in mind, so that all the appropriate skills are available in all settings.

1.17. Some local authorities have developed policies which draw together services for young children and they have set up administrative arrangements for monitoring implementation. The new duty to review day care services involves a process of measurement or assessment, which means that the local authority as a whole should have aims and objectives for services for young children. Local authorities will wish to consider how best to achieve this and what the administrative structure should be.

CHAPTER 2   SERVICE PROVISION

2.1. Section 17 of Part III gives local authorities a general duty to safeguard and promote the welfare of children in need and to promote the upbringing of such children by their families, so far as this is consistent with their welfare duty to the child, by providing an appropriate range and level of services. Schedule 2 contains further provisions designed to help children in need continue to live with their families and generally to prevent the breakdown of family relation-ships. Partnership with parents and consultation with children on the basis of careful joint planning and agreement is the guiding principle for the provision of services within the family home and where children are provided with accommodation under voluntary arrangements. Such arrangements are intended to assist the parent and enhance, not undermine, the parent's authority and control. This new approach should also be developed when a child is in care, provided that it does not jeopardise his welfare.

2.2. Part III also covers the general duty of a local authority towards children being 'looked after'. The term 'looked after' is the new term used in the Act to cover all children accommodated by a local authority, whether by voluntary arrangement or because of a care order. There is more emphasis on the need to make plans for children in partnership with those who are important in the child's life and the child, subject to his understanding, and to involve those people in reviewing such plans.

IN NEED

2.3. Section 17(10) defines 'children in need' as follows:

"For the purposes of this Part a child shall be taken to be in need if:-

(a) he is unlikely to achieve or maintain, or to have the opportunity of achieving or maintaining, a reasonable standard of health or development without the provision for him of services by a local authority under this Part;

(b) his health or development is likely to be significantly impaired, or further impaired, without the provision for him of such services; or

(c) he is disabled,

and "family", in relation to such a child, includes any person who has parental responsibility for the child and any other person with whom he has been living. Section 17(11) explains that for the purpose of this Part, a child is disabled if he is blind, deaf or dumb or suffers from mental disorder of any kind or is substantially and permanently handicapped by illness, injury or congenital deformity or such other disability as may be prescribed; and in this Part —

"development" means physical, intellectual, emotional, social or behavioural development; and

"health" means physical or mental health.'

2.4. The definition of 'need' in the Act is deliberately wide to reinforce the emphasis on preventive support and services to families. It has three categories: a reasonable standard of health or development; significant impairment of health or development; and disablement. It would not be acceptable for an authority to exclude any of these three – for example, by confining services to children at risk of significant harm which attracts the duty to investigate under section 47. The child's needs will include physical, emotional and educational needs according to his age, sex, race, religion, culture and language and the capacity of the current carer to meet those needs. This guidance does not lay down firm criteria or set general priorities because the Act requires each authority to decide their own level and scale of services appropriate to the children in need in their area. However, because the definition is in the Act, a local authority cannot lawfully substitute any other definition for the purposes of Part III.

2.5. In assessing individual need, authorities must assess the existing strengths and skills of the families concerned and help them overcome identified difficulties and enhance strengths. Sometimes the needs will be found to be intrinsic to the child; at other times however it may be that parenting skills and resources are depleted or under-developed and thus threaten the child's well-being. For example, a chronically sick parent may need continuing practical and emotional support of varying degrees of intensity according to the incidence of acute phases of his illness and the developing needs of the child. At times, a sick parent may seek short periods of local authority accommodation for the child so as to have a period of recuperation and avoid stress for the child; in these cases social workers should consider whether a package of support services provided in the home would be the better form of provision. Children should not necessarily be identified as in need because one or both parents are disabled, although this could of course be a factor. It may be that the provision of services to the parent, either under adult disabled persons legislation or under section 17(3) of the Act may safeguard the welfare of the child sufficiently to enable the parent to continue looking after him at home. In other cases social problems, relationship problems, unemployment or bereavement, for example, may temporarily reduce the quality of care of children in the family. A package of support and prompt use of respite care may sustain the child's longer term well-being within the family.

2.6. The Act envisages family support services being offered to members of a family of a child in need where the service is provided with a view to safeguarding and promoting the child's welfare (section 17(3)). Any person who has parental responsibility for the child and any other person with whom the child is living is included so that a local authority may put together a package of services for a family which could include home help, day care provision for a family member other than the child in need (eg another child in the household) or a short-term, temporary placement for the child to relieve the carer. The outcome of any service provision under this power should be evaluated to see whether it has met the primary objective, namely to safeguard or promote the child's welfare.

Assessment

2.7. Good practice requires that the assessment of need should be undertaken in an open way and should involve those caring for the child, the child and other significant persons. Families with a child in need, whether the need results from family difficulties or the child's circumstances, have the right to receive sympathetic support and sensitive intervention in their family's life. Paragraph 3 of Schedule 2 to the Act provides that "a local authority may assess a child's needs for the purpose of this Act at the same time as any assessment under:

(a) the Chronically Sick and Disabled Persons Act 1970;

(b) the Education Act 1981;

(c) the Disabled Persons (Services, Consultation and Representation) Act 1986; or

(d) any other enactment."

2.8. In making an assessment, the local authority should take account of the particular needs of the child – that is in relation to health, development, disability, education, religious persuasion, racial origin, cultural and linguistic background, the degree, (if any) to which these needs are being met by existing services to the family or child and which agencies' services are best suited to the child's needs. In the case of a child with disabilities or a child with a parent with communication difficulties provision of a sign language interpreter, large print, tape and braille may need to be made if communication is to be effective. The need for an interpreter should be considered where the family's first language is not English.

2.9. Assessment must identify and find a way to provide as helpful a guide as possible to the child's needs. Necessary experience and expertise should be provided for in staffing of services and through relationships with other professions and services and with the community. In some areas the local community may include too great a variety of ethnic groups to be reflected fully in composition of staff. In others, local authorities may be called on only rarely to provide a service for a child or family from a minority ethnic group. In both these circumstances, local authorities will need to identify sources of advice and help so that the necessary experience, expertise and resources are available when needed. Care is needed to ensure that the terms 'black' and 'black family' are not used in isolation or in such a way as to obscure characteristics and needs.

Planning a Service for the Individual Child

2.10. Once a need has been identified a plan for the best service provision will be required. This may simply amount to matching the need with an existing service in the community. Where the local authority has to allocate resources to arrange a service – for example, a family aide for the family or a day nursery place for the child – the plan must identify how long the service may be required, what the objective of the service should be and what else others are expected to do. In order to be effective this plan should form the basis of an agreement with the parent or other carer and be reviewed at appropriate intervals. A child, not the subject of a care order, who is provided with a service while living at home is not 'looked after'. However where the local authority is significantly involved with the family good practice means that the requirements in respect of 'looked after' children relating to Arrangements for Placement and Review should also apply to these children.

Meeting Needs

2.11. Section 17 and Part 1 of Schedule 2 to the Act set out in considerable detail the specific duties and powers of the local authorities in relation to support services for children with families. Under section 17(1) local authorities have a general duty to provide a range and level of services appropriate to the children in their area who are 'in need' so as to safeguard and promote their welfare and, so far as is consistent with that aim, promote their upbringing by their families. Local authorities are not expected to meet every individual need, but they are asked to identify the extent of need and then make decisions on the priorities for service provision in their area in the context of that information and their statutory duties. Local authorities will have to ensure that a range of services is available to meet the extent and nature of need identified within their administrative areas. In addition to day care provision for pre-school and school age children, it is likely that a range of services designed to support and improve the strengths and skills of parents in their own homes and neighbourhoods will be required. It is also likely that a vigorous foster care service will be required, offering a range of placements which reflects the racial, cultural, linguistic and religious needs of children requiring accommodation, and is responsive to the amount of short term, longer term, or permanent placements which the children may need. It remains likely that some children will need special forms of resid-ential care. In many areas these services exist already, provided by statutory, voluntary and independent sources. It is important to recognise the benefits of developing packages of services appropriate to the assessed needs of individual children and their families, rather than directing them to existing services which may not be appropriate. Chapter 3 describes the range of services which are likely to be needed but this is not an exhaustive list; others may need to be provided according to the local authority's assessment of need in their own area.

2.12. Local authorities are also expected to act as facilitators of provision of the services covered by section 17, 18 (day care) and 20, 23 (accommodation) and 24 (advice and assistance to certain young persons aged under 21) by others as well as being the principal providers themselves (section 17(5)). They must publicise the availability of such services and they should monitor and evaluate the availability of all those services which can be viewed as family support. In undertaking these tasks the local authority will have to ensure that they are properly informed about the different racial groups to which children within their area who are in need belong (paragraph 11 of Schedule 2.) The development of information systems will assist local authorities in this task. When they have assembled the information they will be able to decide on priorities and allocate resources for services such as family support, day care and fostering and consider how to deal with the consequential staffing and recruitment issues. Local authorities should provide a range of services which should reflect (in scale as well as type) the needs of children and families from ethnic minority groups. More detailed guidance on issues of race and culture and placement of children is contained in volume 3 in this series (Family Placements).

CHANGE OF EMPHASIS

2.13. The effect of the provision of services to support families may often be to avoid the need to take the child into long-term compulsory care. Section 1 of the Child Care Act 1980 was formulated in a way that implied that the aim of supportive work is to prevent admission to care. This has contributed to a negative interpretation of local authority interaction with families. The direct link between preventive work and reducing the need for court procedures found in section 1 of the Child Care Act 1980 is reproduced in the Children Act in paragraph 7 of Schedule 2 but only as one of a range of local authority duties and powers. The accommodation of a child by a local authority is now to be viewed as a service providing positive support to a child and his family.

2.14. In general, families have the capacity to cope with their own problems, or to identify and draw upon resources in the community for support. Some families however reach a stage where they are not able to resolve their own difficulties, and are therefore providing inadequate care for their child or are afraid of doing so. They may look to social services for support and assistance. If they do this they should receive a positive response which reduces any fears they may have of stigma or loss of parental responsibility.

2.15 The Act gives a positive emphasis to identifying and providing for the child's needs rather than focusing on parental shortcomings in a negative manner. The responsibility on local authorities to provide accommodation for children in need who require it – because, for example, the parents are prevented from providing appropriate care during the illness of one parent – replaces 'reception into care' with its unhelpful associations of parental shortcomings. Where, for example, parents who usually provide good and devoted care for their child need a break, the provision of additional help in the home or suitable accommodation for the child for a short time should be seen as a service to the child and family without pressure or prejudice. Children accommodated are 'looked after' by the local authority in partnership with the parents. The Act also emphasises that partnership with parents should not become weaker if it becomes necessary to provide the child with accommodation.

2.16. In putting together packages of services, local authorities should take account of services provided by the voluntary sector and other agencies. Some examples of supportive services provided under section 17 are advice on such matters as local facilities, social security benefits, housing or education, domiciliary support in the form of family aides, befriending schemes, play facilities and specialist services such as counselling, parent-craft training, family centres, respite care and the provision of accommodation for longer periods. In appropriate circumstances assistance given may be in kind or, exceptionally, in cash (section 17(6)).

2.17. The definition of a disabled child in section 17(11) of the Act is:

"A child is disabled if he is blind, deaf or dumb or suffers from mental disorder of any kind or is substantially and permanently handicapped by illness, injury or congenital deformity or such other disability as may be prescribed."

The definition is that used for adults under the National Assistance Act 1948 and covers children affected by physical disability, chronic sickness, mental disability, sensory disability, communication impairment, and mental illness.

2.18. The Act places a clear, positive and separate duty on local authorities to provide services for children with disabilities within their area so as to minimise the effect of their disabilities and give such children the opportunity to lead lives which are as normal as possible (Schedule 2, paragraph 6). These services should help in the identification, diagnosis, assessment and treatment of children with physical and mental handicaps, or suffering from mental disorder and help those children in their adjustment to handicap, and in overcoming limitations of mobility and communication in appropriate ways. This may include the funding and provision of equipment such as communication aids and interpreters. Authorities will need to consider in co-operation with the relevant agencies the child's overall developmental needs – physical, social, intellectual, emotional and behavioural – when considering what sort of services are required.

Registration of Children with Disabilities

2.19. The Act also continues but separates out the requirement placed on local authorities to keep registers of children with disabilities in their area (Schedule 2 paragraph 2). This provision, which is designed to help their service planning and monitoring, originated from directions made under the National Assistance Act 1948 in relation to disabled persons; if the register is to be of maximum use and benefit it has to be complete and avoid duplication with other registers. It is suggested that local authorities in conjunction with local education authorities and health authorities draw up a common register to assist collaboration and for use in their respective areas of responsibility. Local authorities should try to establish a system, particularly with local education and health authorities, for identifying the number and needs of children in their areas who are disabled through physical, sensory or mental disablement, mental disorders and chronic illness so that they may jointly plan their services for the short and long term. Registration is voluntary on the part of parents and children and not a precondition of service provision, but local authorities, in collaboration with health authorities, local education authorities and voluntary agencies in their area, need to publicise widely and positively the existence and purpose of registers to relevant professionals, parents and young people. The publicity should stress the usefulness of the register as an aid to planning the right level and mix of local services to help parents with children with disabilities. In the longer term, the register will also assist in planning services for when the children become adults. Registration should be encouraged for these reasons and on the grounds that it may improve access to other agency resources such as those provided in the voluntary sector and financial benefits such as social security benefits, tax relief (if registered blind) or assistance with text telephones (if registered deaf). Efforts made to keep accurate and comprehensive registers and to encourage registration will help to ensure that children with disabilities gain access to the services for which the Act makes provision.

2.20. Apart from the Children Act, the Chronically Sick and Disabled Persons Act 1970 and the Disabled Persons (Services, Consultation and Representation) Act 1986 (as amended by the Children Act) confer additional functions on local authorities in respect of children with disabilities. (The relevant circulars are LAO(87)6 and LAC(88)2). These Acts also apply to adults and deal mainly with matters of wider application to both adults and children such as the type of welfare services to be provided and the assessments of need for such services.

2.21. Under Schedule 2, paragraph 3 of the Act, local authorities have the power to arrange for any assessment of a child with a disability because he may be in need, to be combined with any assessment under the Chronically Sick and Disabled Persons Act 1970, the Education Act 1981 (for special educational needs), the Disabled Persons (Services, Consultation and Representation) Act 1986 or any other enactment. In the past assessments have tended to be undertaken separately by the relevant departments. Health authorities, for example, have a key role in assessment, particularly for children with disabilities. Co-ordination may on occasion have been ineffective between health and local authorities or between different departments of the same authority. This Act makes it possible to bring together in one process assessment for several different services where this is appropriate and in the child's best interests. Such collaboration should in future ensure that all authorities see children 'in the round', whether their particular needs are for educational or health or social care. It should ensure that parents and children are not subject to a confusing variety of assessment procedures. Assessment should be less an administrative process for a single department and more an opportunity for a local authority to co-ordinate all services effectively. More detailed guidance on working with children with disabilities in the context of the Children Act is in a separate volume in this series.

Integration of Services

2.22. The new emphasis on integration of services for children with disabilities with those provided for other children in need has the effect that, in addition to the duty under Schedule 2, paragraph 6 to provide services, local authorities must offer children with disabilities accommodated by them or by other agencies, the benefit of those powers and duties which they have in respect of all children whom they look after. Requirements such as having to review the case of a child who has been living away from home, having to give paramount consideration to his welfare and to consult him and his parents before decisions are taken, therefore, apply to children with disabilities as well as other children in need, without any loss of any special provisions that applied to children with disabilities prior to implementation of the Children Act. This is a change from the old law where a child with a disability only benefited from the welfare provision if 'received or taken into care' by a local authority.

CHILDREN LIVING WITH THEIR FAMILIES

2.23. Paragraph 8 of Schedule 2 requires local authorities to make such provision as they consider appropriate so that the following services are available for children in need in their area.

- advice, guidance and counselling;
- occupational, social, cultural and recreational activities;
- home help (including laundry facilities);
- facilities or assistance with travelling to and from any services provided under the Act or any similar service;
- assistance to enable the child and the family to have a holiday;

It is important to have regard to this general duty when planning a service for an individual child.

PROVISION OF ACCOMMODATION

2.24. The Act intends accommodation to be provided as a service under voluntary arrangements which parents with a child in need may seek to take up so long as it is in the best interests of the child. Section 20(1) of the Act states that:

"Every local authority shall provide accommodation for any child in need within their area who appears to them to require accommodation as a result of:-

(a) there being no person who has parental responsibility for him;

(b) his being lost or having been abandoned; or

(c) the person who has been caring for him being prevented (whether or not permanently, and for whatever reason) from providing him with suitable accommodation or care."

2.25. The Act assumes a high degree of co-operation between parents and local authorities in negotiating and agreeing what form of accommodation can be offered and the use to be made of it. The accommodated child is not in care (unless subject to a care order) and there is no provision which allows a local authority to take over parental rights administratively as was the case under Section 3 of the 1980 Act. Therefore parents are able to remove a child from accommodation whenever they wish to do so. As stated above local authorities are required to provide accommodation for a child in need who "appears to them to require accommodation" (section 20(1)). In the case of a child aged over 16 this requirement applies in exceptional circumstances (section 20(3)) but general powers in sections 20(4) and 20(5) permit local authorities to accommodate over 16s.

2.26. The Act makes no distinction between requirements applying to the provision of a series of pre-planned short-term placements and longer-term provision of accommodation. This is because in practice differences in the provision of a service are not easily sustained. In every voluntary arrangement the service should be based on a voluntary decision by the parents to take up an appropriate service on offer and continuing parental participation in and agreement to the arrangements for the child. If there is no one with parental responsibility and no suitable carer the local authority will need to consider how best to provide the child with someone to exercise parental responsibility. This may mean that the local authority should assist another appropriate person to obtain a residence order for the child; as in providing accommodation for a child the local authority has certain duties but does not take over parental responsibility. Thus, under section 3(5) of the Act local authorities (or others) caring for a child, but without parental responsibility may do what is reasonable in each individual case to safeguard or promote the child's welfare. This may happen as a result of the child's request or on the local authority's initiative.

Nature of Arrangement

2.27. In the provision of services the emphasis will be on partnership with the child's family so as to provide for the child's needs by voluntary arrangement, build upon the family's strengths and minimise any weaknesses. This is reflected in the provisions in the Act relating to service provision and voluntarily agreed arrangements. Parents can no longer be legally required to give notice before withdrawing their children from voluntary arrangements and authorities are no longer able to assume parental rights over children by administrative resolution. Review of the service provision will be necessary to check that the objective is being met. Every effort should be made to enhance the parents' capabilities and confidence so that they may provide effectively for the child's welfare. However, the nature of the voluntary arrangement should not prevent a continuing assessment of any risk to the child; and where the circumstances require it, the child protection procedures should be brought into play immediately (see volume 1 in this series and **Working Together**).

Partnership

2.28. Partnership requires informed participation. The Act therefore requires that parents and children must be consulted during the decision-making process and notified of the outcome. There is a new requirement placed on local authorities to establish a procedure for considering representations (including complaints) about the discharge of their functions under this part of the Act. The

Act emphasises that, where possible, children should participate in decision-making about their future well-being. Subject only to the child's understanding, such participation requires that a child is provided with relevant information and is consulted at every stage in the process of decision-making.

Partnership or Compulsion

2.29 The provision of services as a means of avoiding compulsory intervention by the courts is provided for in Schedule 2 paragraphs 4(1) and 5 and 7. The Act affirms the key principle that a court order should not be made unless the court considers this the most effective way of safeguarding or promoting the child's welfare. This places emphasis on action to reduce the need for children to be in care. When an emergency arises, the Act clarifies local authorities' power to provide accommodation away from the family home for an adult, who is deemed to be a risk to the child, and who is willing to leave so as to save the child the trauma of removal. This will be one of the child protection issues on which staff will need guidance and the policy on priority of resources in this context needs to be clear. Staff will also need training and guidance on the complex issue of weighing the viability and value of a voluntary arrangement against potential risk and the best interests of the child. (Child protection matters are dealt with in volume 1 in this series and **Working Together**).

2.30 In a case where a child is suffering or is likely to suffer significant harm (as defined in section 31(9) and (10) of the Act) the local authority has to decide whether provision of accommodation by agreement with the parents is sufficient to safeguard the welfare of the child or whether application for a care or supervision order is appropriate. In the majority of cases local authorities will be able to agree on an arrangement that will best provide for the needs of the child and safeguard and promote his welfare. Work with parents to achieve an initial agreement to the accommodation of the child by the local authority will usually ensure that the ongoing plan for the child can be operated in partnership with his parents. Where a parent is unwilling to co-operate at the outset or becomes unco-operative or inconsistent in attitude or commitment to the child the nature of the arrangement should be reassessed and the need for care proceedings or emergency protection action should be considered. If the court refuses an application for a care order, the local authority will have to decide whether seeking to reach a voluntary arrangement would be an appropriate alternative. If, in any family proceedings where the court has directed the local authority to investigate the child's circumstances, the local authority decides not to apply for a care or supervision order, it will have to explain this decision to the court (section 37). The reaching of an agreement on a voluntary arrangement to meet the child's needs would be a relevant consideration.

IN NEED, AWAY FROM HOME BUT NOT LOOKED AFTER

2.31. Where a child in need in the local authority's area is living apart from his family the local authority must consider whether or not they should exercise their duty under Schedule 2 paragraph 10. This requires the local authority to take such steps as are reasonably practicable, if they consider it necessary to do so in order to safeguard or promote a child's welfare, where any child within their area who is in need and whom they are not looking after is living apart from his family. The steps mentioned in the Act are to enable him to live with his family or to promote contact between him and his family.

AFTERCARE

2.32. The continuum of care provided by a good parent does not cease at any arbitrary point, but it changes to meet the different needs of a child over time and continues to be available to a young adult, away from the family home but in need of support and advice from time to time. In acknowledgement of this the Act extends local authorities' responsibilities for young people leaving care and includes those previously accommodated by health or local education authorities, voluntary organisations and in private children's homes. This applies where no suitable arrangements are made by those agencies and also to privately fostered children. This provision of support, advice and assistance which has tended to be known as 'leaving care', is to be called 'aftercare', which reflects better the intention of the Act. Aftercare includes advice, general help and moral support, financial assistance in exceptional circumstances and specific financial assistance in connection with employment, education or training. Planning aftercare services for individual children will help the child to adjust during the transition from child to adult and will allow the local authority and other responsible agencies to arrange in good time any new service that may be required.

Contact and re-unification

2.33.   The Act requires local authorities to promote contact between a child who is being looked after and all those who are connected with the child unless it is not reasonably practicable or consistent with the child's welfare. The Act also firmly addresses the re-unification of a child with his family. These are linked issues. If contact is not maintained re-unification becomes less likely and recognition of this has to underpin all considerations in planning for a child.

CHILDREN LOOKED AFTER IN OTHER ESTABLISHMENTS

2.34. Local authorities have a new welfare duty in respect of a child accommodated (for a consecutive period of more than three months) by a health or local education authority, by a residential care, nursing or mental nursing home or in an independent school (sections 85-87). This requires them to take reasonable steps to enable them to decide, whether the child's welfare is adequately safeguarded and promoted while staying in the accommodation. (See separate guidance in this series.)

PUBLICISING SERVICES

2.35. Local authorities have a duty under Schedule 2, paragraph 1(2) to publicise the services available to families with children in need under Part III of the Act and to take such steps as are reasonably practicable to ensure that those who might benefit from the services receive the information. This supplements the duty local authorities have under section 1 of the Chronically Sick and Disabled Persons Act 1970, to inform people with disabilities, on request, of relevant services provided by the local authority or an organisation of which particulars are in the local authority's possession. This means that local authorities should publish information about the services they provide themselves and, where appropriate, those provided by others.

2.36. Any publicity materials produced should take account of ethnic minorities' cultural and linguistic needs and the needs of those with sensory disabilities in the audience to whom the materials are addressed. As far as possible, the relevant publicity should encourage parents to seek help if it is needed. Some potential applicants are likely to be wary of invoking official involvement in their lives. Sensitive publicity material can minimise these concerns.

2.37. This new duty is likely to increase interest in and awareness of the importance of information about services for parents in helping them bring up their children and make informed choices about use of facilities in the area.

CHARGING FOR SERVICES

2.38. Local authorities should ensure that their policy on charging for services and requiring contributions towards the cost of accommodating a child is clearly stated and understood by staff, and that information about the policy is made available to all concerned. Services and assistance provided under section 17(7) may be unconditional or subject to conditions as to the repayment of the assistance or its value. In planning service provision and resource allocation the local authority must have regard to sections 17(8) and (9) which state:

"(8) Before giving any assistance or imposing any conditions, a local authority shall have regard to the means of the child concerned and of each of his parents.

(9) No person shall be liable to make any repayment of assistance or of its value at any time when he is in receipt of income support or family credit under the Social Security Act 1986."

2.39. Local authorities are given discretion to decide whether or not to impose reasonable charges for services, assistance in kind, or cash provided under Part III of the Act (section 29(1)). This is not new. In deciding whether or not to impose charges, local authorities should bear in mind that in some cases parents may accept the provision of services more readily if they are given the opportunity to contribute to the cost. Others may be deterred from seeking support before a crisis if their liability for repayment is unclear. Information on the local authority's policy should be available to the public.

2.40. A local authority which is looking after a child must consider whether or not to recover contributions towards the cost of the child's maintenance from a parent of the child or, when he is sixteen, the child himself. The only exceptions to this are where a child is looked after under an interim care order, an emergency protection order (or any other provision of Part V) or certain other criminal provisions (Schedule 2, paragraph 21). Contributions may only be recovered when the authority considers it reasonable to do so and not at all from a person who is in receipt of Income Support or Family Credit or while the child is allowed to live with a parent of his. (Schedule 2, paragraph 21(2)-(4)).

2.41. The procedure for recovery of contributions for services including accommodation has been simplified since the Child Care Act 1980. The local authority which wants to receive contributions must serve a contribution notice on the contributor, specifying a weekly sum not greater than that which the authority would be prepared to pay foster parents for looking after a similar child and which it is reasonable to expect the contributor to pay. The notice must also state the proposed arrangements for payment (Schedule 2, paragraph 22). If the contributor does not agree with the sum and arrangements for payment (as specified in the notice or otherwise proposed by the authority), or if he withdraws his agreement, the authority may apply to court for a contribution order. This order may not specify a sum greater than that which was in the contribution notice. If the contributor and the local authority agree the terms of a new contribution notice, this will discharge an existing contribution order. Failing agreement, a contribution order may be varied or discharged on the application of the contributor or the local authority (Schedule 2, paragraph 23).

CHAPTER 3   RANGE OF SERVICES

3.1. Local authorities are given a general duty under the Act to promote the upbringing of children by their families (section 17(1)). In support of this duty local authorities are given a number of related duties in respect of family support services. They are required to make provision for advice, guidance, counselling, assistance and home help services. They are empowered to provide social, cultural or leisure activities or assistance with holidays (Schedule 2). Local authorities are required, in addition to provide such family centres as they consider appropriate in relation to the children in their area.

3.2. Every authority is required to take reasonable steps through the provision of Part III services to prevent children in their area suffering ill-treatment or neglect. A local authority is required to inform another authority if a child, whom the authority believes is likely to suffer harm, lives or proposes to live in the area of that authority: (Schedule 2, paragraph 4.) There is a connected duty to take reasonable steps, (through provision of Part III services,) to reduce the need to bring proceedings for care or supervision orders, family or other proceedings which might lead to placement in care, High Court proceedings under the inherent jurisdiction or criminal proceedings in respect of children. Authorities should also encourage children not to commit criminal offences and avoid the need for placing them in secure accommodation. (Schedule 2, paragraph 6). These provisions bring together the duties placed on local authorities to offer services to families which may break up without the provision of services. In addition, in the child protection context, if it appears to an authority that a child is suffering or is likely to suffer ill-treatment at the hands of another person living at the same premises and that person proposes to move from those premises, the authority may assist that other person to obtain alternative accommodation, including assistance in cash (Schedule 2 paragraphs 5)

DAY CARE SERVICES

3.3. Chapters 4 to 9 in this volume give detailed guidance on development of services, standards to be met in different types of services, and the registration, inspection and review functions. That part of the guidance applies to day care services in general but there are particular considerations in relation to children in need and their use of day care. These are dealt with here but local authorities should also take account of the guidance in Chapters 4 to 9.

3.4. Local authorities should have an agreed policy for discharging their general duty to provide day care for children in need. This should involve examining day care services for children in need in the wider context of the services used by all children, so that children in need have similar opportunities for developing skills and interests. They should have regard to section 17(5) of the Act which requires them in the discharge of their duties under Part III to facilitate provision of services by other organisations including voluntary bodies and the private sector and Schedule 2 paragraph II(a) which confers a duty to consider the racial groups to which children in need belong when making arrangements for the provision of day care.

3.5. In considering whether or not to offer day care services for children in need, local authorities should ensure that full consideration is given to the views of parents and children. The Act gives local authorities a duty to do this in respect of the children they look after and this should, as a matter of good practice, also be applied in respect of children in need who are being cared for by their parents.

3.6. There should be a variety of day care facilities in the area so that there is some choice for children in need and they can attend the one which best meets their needs. Where a local authority decides to offer day care for a child in need, the parents should be involved in the discussion about the type of day care service and their views should be respected. Wherever possible local authorities should arrange for a child in need to go to the day care service which the parents prefer so long as that accords with the child's needs and best interests. They should also, where appropriate, have regard to the views of the child.

3.7. Local authorities may discharge their general duty to provide day care for children in need either through their own provision or by making arrangements to use facilities run by independent providers such as voluntary organisation or private firms or individuals. In some cases it will be better for the children and more cost effective to use an independent service. It may also mean that children attend a facility which is in the area where they live or go to school. They will therefore be with children from their own community or neighbourhood.

Day Nurseries

3.8. Attendance at a day nursery provides opportunities for children in need to take part in group activity with their peers. Activities and learning experiences are planned by skilled staff and will enhance development of children's skills. It is for each local authority to decide on their policy about using day nurseries for children in need who are under two. In many if not all cases it may be considered that childminding is more appropriate because a childminder provides care on an individual basis in a domestic setting. However, where, for example, an older sibling is already attending a day nursery and there is concern about parenting skills, a place for the younger child may be in his best interests.

Playgroups

3.9. Attendance at playgroup will give children in need opportunities to take part in group activity with their peers who probably come from the same neighbourhood. The philosophy of the playgroup movement is based on the premise that parents are fully involved in the running of a group although most groups employ one or two paid staff. Arranging a playgroup place for a child in need may offer a means of helping parents improve their parenting skills because the involvement will show how parents contribute to the child's development. This will need careful planning and discussion with the playgroup organisers who will need to have proper support in order to help. Local authorities, in developing their policies on day care services for children in need, should also consider the value of sponsoring places in playgroups and facilitating the development of new groups as part of their wider responsibilities for parents and children in need, including children with disabilities under the Act.

Childminding

3.10. Some local authorities already run sponsored childminding schemes or employ childminders who look after children aged under five in order to help families with health or social difficulties. Children receive individual care in a domestic setting and this may provide an effective way of supporting parents with a child in need, particularly where he is very young. Local authorities should provide adequate support for childminders with whom they place such children. This might include training opportunities, access to specialised equipment, regular visits from social services staff and counselling. Local authorities should ensure that any package of family support which includes placing children in need with childminders also recognises the importance of group activities, particularly for 3 and 4 year olds, so that arrangements are made for attendance at some form of group facility such as playgroup or nursery class. Close arrangements between a nursery and a group of childminders can be helpful.

Out-of-School Clubs and Holiday Schemes

3.11. These services have an important preventive function because they look after children who might otherwise become 'latchkey children', be at risk of being harmed or becoming delinquent. Local authorities may wish to consider setting up new clubs or supporting existing ones as a community resource to help them discharge their duties under Schedule 2, paragraphs 4 and 7 (prevention of neglect and abuse and reducing the need for care proceedings). This might also involve discussing the benefits of such services with the local education authority and school governors. Apart from its preventive role, attendance at a club or holiday scheme provides opportunities for children to develop leisure interests. Where it is decided that it is appropriate for children in need to attend an out-of-school club or holiday scheme, local authorities should take account of the children's views and where possible, arrange for them to go to their preferred club or scheme. Where it is decided to use independently run clubs or holiday schemes for children in need local authorities should ensure that the workers are properly supported. This might include regular visits, access to training, specialised equipment or counselling.

Supervised Activities

3.12. This term, which is part of day care, describes activities which might not otherwise be seen as care especially in the case of school age children. They may be focused on a particular interest for example Red Cross, St John Ambulance, bird watching, sports club. Attendance at such activities may help children in need develop particular skills which enhance their confidence and self- esteem as well as allowing them to take part in a wider range of activities. Local authorities should bear this in mind when developing their day care policies for children in need.

Befriending Services

3.13. A befriending scheme will recruit and train volunteers (who typically are more experienced parents) who help a parent under stress and having difficulty coping with young children. They usually involve regular visits to the family in the home. This type of service has been successfully developed by Home-Start Consultancy which provides support and advice to autonomous local schemes in many parts of the country. Data collected about use of the schemes show that referrals come mainly from health visitors or social workers with a few self-referrals. Other befriending services such as those run by NEWPIN may also offer opportunities for parents to take part in group activities in order to lessen feelings of isolation, improve parents' insight into their difficulties and develop skills. There are some educational home visiting services attached to schools. Portage schemes have also developed in many areas as a means of helping parents bring up children with disabilities. All these befriending services offer parents under stress significant amounts of time from volunteers who are likely to be seen as friends with no power or tradition of interfering in family life and who may themselves have surmounted similar difficulties to those met by the family being visited. Where staff working in local or health authorities identify at an early stage that a parent may have difficulty in coping with a young child or children referral to a befriending service can offer an effective preventive service. However, it is important that such referrals are monitored and, where appropriate, the volunteers properly supported.

Parent/Toddler Groups

3.14. A parent/toddler group or one o'clock club may meet once or twice a week for one or two hours. These are usually run on a self-help basis, sometimes attached to a playgroup. The parent or carer stays with the child but most groups will also have one or two paid people to organise sessions. Groups provide opportunities for parents and carers to meet others with children of a similar age and share their experiences. The children will be able to take part in different play activities – painting, water play, messy play, use of construction toys, climbing equipment or trundle toys. Local authorities should consider how to encourage parents with children in need to attend groups as a means of providing opportunities to meet others in their community and to become more confident about their ability to cope. Some parents may be reluctant to attend a group through lack of confidence or low self-esteem. Discussion with group organisers may be necessary in order to identify how to encourage them to attend, perhaps by arranging for another parent to bring them to the group.

Toy Libraries

3.15. These may be run by social services departments, health authorities, schools or voluntary groups. Many provide toys specially designed to help children with disabilities or those with learning difficulties. Toy libraries will usually be able to advise parents about the type of toy which will help children develop particular skills and will also help a parent learn about suitable toys for different ages and stages. Most toy libraries are open once or twice a week and may make a small charge for borrowing toys. Generally children can experiment with the toy before taking it home. Some toy libraries also offer play sessions. There are a few mobile toy libraries and in some areas the toy librarian will visit families in their homes. Toy libraries are places where parents can obtain informal advice about play, toys and child development. They provide access to a wide and changing range of toys and for more disadvantaged families this can help extend the learning experiences of their children.

Drop-in Centres

3.16. These have evolved in recent years to provide an informal open door for parents and children. Some may be targeted on particular types of family (for example those living in temporary accommodation, particular ethnic groups, lone parents), others may be neighbourhood based. They may be managed by statutory bodies, self-help groups or voluntary bodies. Some may combine the drop-in element with playgroup sessions or keep fit classes or they may be part of other facilities – for example, family centres.

Playbuses

3.17. These are usually double decker buses converted to provide space for groups to meet and take part in particular activities. Some are managed by statutory authorities, others by voluntary groups. Apart from being used by parents with under fives, they may also cater for retired or unemployed people, or people with disabilities or teenagers. Playbuses are a particularly useful resource in sparsely populated rural areas or isolated parts of cities. They can also provide a service for families who have difficulty reaching other facilities.

FAMILY CENTRES

3.18. Paragraph 9 of Schedule 2 gives local authorities a general duty 'to provide such family centres as they consider appropriate in relation to children within their area'. The Act defines family centres as places where a child, his parents and anyone who has parental responsibility for or is looking after him may go for occupational, social, cultural, or recreational activities or advice, guidance or counselling or the person may be accommodated whilst he is receiving advice, guidance and counselling.

3.19. This general duty is not confined to children in need. Local authorities should decide whether to discharge this duty through providing such facilities themselves or facilitating other organisations to do so. If they have not already done so, they should establish what family centres there are in their area, the type of services each provides and how they are used. This might be done in conjunction with the process of identifying children in need and publishing information about local authority services and those provided by other organisations (paragraph 1 of Schedule 2) and when reviewing the day care services used by children aged under 8 in the area (section 19).

3.20. Family centres may be run by local authorities or voluntary bodies. There are three main types:

(a) **Therapeutic**

In these, skilled workers carry out intensive casework with families experiencing severe difficulties with the aim of improving the ability to function as a family and relationships between parents and children or between siblings. Some such centres provide accommodation to do this. Many local authorities have adopted a policy of using former day nurseries and residential children's homes as family centres where services are offered to the family as a unit in order to improve parenting. Day care may be offered for under fives and there will usually be a range of other services offered such as playgroup sessions, toy libraries, pre-employment and skills training, marriage guidance, child health clinics, or out of school clubs.

(b) **Community**

Local voluntary groups including churches may provide a neighbourhood based facility for parents to use as a meeting place and take part in particular activities. These may also offer such activities as playgroup sessions, parent/toddler groups, toy libraries, adult education classes.

(c) **Self-help**

These may be run as a co-operative venture by a community group and are likely to offer various support services for families in an informal and unstructured way.

3.21. Local authorities should consider whether family centres of the therapeutic type would provide an effective way of discharging some of their Part III duties. In particular, attendance at a family centre might form one element of a package of services put together for a family with a child in need. These facilities, unlike the others described in this chapter, provide a place where parents and children of all ages can go and for this reason they may be suitable for a wide range of families. They also provide a place where adult members of a family can go to take part in activities which may help to improve their confidence and their ability to cope more effectively with their difficulties.

3.22. They may provide accommodation where families can be observed for prolonged periods which may help to identify particular difficulties with parenting skills and what action to take to improve family function. They may also provide a setting where the children can be looked after whilst the parents are discussing their difficulties. A family centre with residential accommodation may be used in other ways apart from intensive case work involving the whole family. It might include offering accommodation to disruptive children for short spells or to one or other of the parents in order to work intensively with an individual member of a family or to prevent family breakdown.

3.23. Other types of family centre are more likely to encourage community involvement and development of facilities for families on a geographical basis. Where local authorities are concerned about families with children who are living in a poor environment, it may be desirable to encourage the setting up of a neighbourhood facility for all local families to use, perhaps involving voluntary organisations.

3.24. Local authorities should ensure that their policy on family centres is developed in line with that for children in need and it forms part of the material assembled in the exercise of the new duty to review day care services used by under 8s.

ACCOMMODATION

3.25. Under section 20(1) local authorities must provide accommodation for a child in need in their area where there is no-one with parental responsibility for him, or he has been lost or abandoned, or the person caring for him is prevented (whether or not permanently and for whatever reason) from providing him with suitable accommodation or care. Section 20(3) gives local authorities a duty to provide accommodation for children aged 16 and 17 if the authority considers their welfare will be seriously prejudiced without such a service. Section 20(4) gives them discretion to provide accommodation for any child if they consider it would safeguard or promote his welfare (even if the person with parental responsibility is prepared to accommodate him). Under section 20(5) they also have power to accommodate 16-21 year olds in community homes (provided the home takes over 16 year olds) if it will safeguard and promote the young person's welfare. Children who are accommodated are referred to as 'looked after' by the local authority and the duty to 'accommodate' a child replaces the duty in the Child Care Act 1980 (section 2) to receive a child into 'voluntary care'. Accommodation in this context relates to the provision of care and maintenance for the child. Section 23(2) of the Children Act points up the Act's specific meaning of 'accommodation' by setting out ways in which the local authority may meet their duty to accommodate.

3.26. The Act also empowers local authorities to assist an adult deemed to be a risk to a child and who is willing to leave so as to save the child the trauma of removal, to obtain accommodation away from the family home. (Schedule 2 Paragraph 5).

Duty to Collaborate

3.27. It is emphasised that the obligation to fulfil these requirements in the Act rests with the social services department of a local authority. However, section 27 requires co-operation between a local social services authority and other authorities which has implications for housing authorities. Section 27 states:

"1. Where it appears to a local authority that any authority mentioned in subsection (3) could, by taking any specified action, help in the exercise of any of their functions under this Part, they may request the help of the other authority, specifying the action in question.

2. An authority whose help is so requested shall comply with the request if it is compatible with their own statutory or other duties and obligations and does not unduly prejudice the discharge of any of their functions.

3. The persons are -
    (a) any local authority;
    (b) any local education authority;
    (c) any local housing authority;
    (d) any health authority; and
    (e) any person authorised by the Secretary of State for the purposes of this section."

Agreement of Arrangements

3.28. The provision of accommodation for a child under a voluntary arrangement is a service voluntarily taken up by parents and it is therefore inappropriate to require them to give a period of notice of their intention to remove the child. The provisions in section 13 of the Child Care Act 1980 (28 days notice of removal is required after six months accommodation of a child) are not reproduced because such a requirement would undermine the voluntary nature of the arrangements between parents and a local authority. However sensible arrangements (recorded in the written agreement) need to be made between the local authority and parent to cover appropriate ways of terminating use of the service that will not mitigate against the child's best interests. Parents who are seeking to agree arrangements in their child's best interests will appreciate the need to minimise disruption to the child. This will be one aspect of the arrangements to be discussed when reaching agreement about a placement. The agreement should be framed so as to enhance the parents' role in their child's life. (See volumes 3 and 4 in this series.)

3.29. As a general rule the local authority may not look after the child by providing accommodation if the parent or person with parental responsibility is acting in the best interests of the child and is able and willing to provide or arrange for the child's accommodation independently. There are two exceptions to this. It does not apply if a person in whose favour a residence order has been made with respect to the child, or a person who has care of the child under an order made in the exercise of the High Court's inherent jurisdiction with respect to children (section 20(7) and (9)) agrees to the provision of accommodation. This may occur when someone else asks for accommodation to be provided – for example the child – or if the local authority itself suggests that this would be in the interests of the welfare of the child. If more than one person has the benefit of a residence order or has care of the child under an inherent jurisdiction order, they must all agree to the child being looked after by the local authority (section 20(10)). If the parent who has a residence order in his favour agrees to the provision of accommodation, the parent without the residence order cannot object to accommodation being provided or remove the child, and if he wished to take over care of the child he would have to get the residence order discharged. If the child has reached sixteen, accommodation may be provided despite parental objection, provided that the child requests and/or agrees to it (section 20(11)).

3.30. The provision of accommodation by agreement is to be viewed as a service to the parents who, in the best interests of their child, voluntarily agree to the arrangements before accommodation is provided. In addition, so far as it is reasonably practicable and consistent with the child's welfare, the local authority must ascertain the child's wishes about provision of accommodation and give due consideration to such wishes as they have been able to ascertain, having regard to his understanding (section 20(6)). This requirement must be kept in mind when planning arrangements for the child.

3.31. A local authority has a number of choices when considering whether to accommodate a child. The options are foster care, a placement in a residential establishment or some other appropriate arrangement (such as semi-independent living for an older child). This accommodation may be provided directly by the local authority or by another agency, for example, a voluntary organisation, on its behalf. The importance of the assessment of need being made in consultation with the child, his parents or anyone else (such as a relative) who was looking after the child before the authority provides accommodation cannot be over-emphasised: it is a statutory duty under section 22(4). (Some guidance on assessment is in **Protecting children – A Guide for Social Workers Undertaking a Comprehensive Assessment (HMSO 1988).**) Planning for the child's immediate care and future welfare based on a full assessment of need in partnership with all concerned will be fundamental to the appropriate provision of accommodation.

3.32. The basis on which the arrangements are made must involve consultations about placement of the child and discussions about local authority plans for him with all those involved with the child or in the plan. Agreements reached will need to involve all those with parental responsibility and will require careful negotiation. The plan for the arrangements will set out (amongst other things) the reasons for, purpose and anticipated length of the child's stay in local authority accommodation (or accommodation provided by other agencies on behalf of the local authority), the arrangements for contact with the child and any delegation of parental responsibility which may be necessary. In a voluntary arrangement the local authority should explain that it will usually be in the child's interests for his return to be planned by all those concerned and that termination of the arrangement should be undertaken in that spirit wherever possible, in accordance with a planned timetable. (See also **The Care of Children – Principles and Practice in Regulations and Guidance) (HMSO 1990).**

REUNIFICATION

3.33. When the local authority is looking after a child, it is required to make arrangements for the child to live with a member of his family unless to do so would be impracticable or inconsistent with the child's welfare (section 23(6)). Family in this context means any person falling within the scope of section 23(4) of the Act or a relative, friend or other significant person in the child's life. This requirement is intended to ensure that the Act's emphasis on the promotion of the upbringing of children within or by their families is applied equally to all children looked after by the local authority. The duties in Schedule 2 paragraph 8 (provision for children living with their families) and paragraph 10 (maintenance of the family home) could be used together to achieve reunification of a family when the child is living apart from some or all of his family but is not looked after by the local authority. This could also be considered when a local authority is notified about a child being accommodated by a health or local education authority or others. The same emphasis on the importance of family links is found in the requirements that a child should be accommodated near his family home (section 23(7)(a)) and that brothers and sisters be accommodated together as long as this is practicable and consistent with each child's welfare (section 23(7)(b)).

SUPPORT SERVICES FOR WORKERS AND PARENTS

3.34. Section 18(3) gives local authorities power to provide facilities such as training, advice, guidance and counselling to people working in a day care setting (including childminding), and anyone who stays with the children while they are attending the service. This power is not limited to providing services for people working with or accompanying children in need. It enables local authorities to help people working in day care and childminders raise their standards and to help parents, those with parental responsibility and those looking after children to improve their parenting skills.

Training

3.35. Local authorities should develop an agreed policy about the extent to which they wish to use this power as part of their policies on family support, day care and educational provision for young children. In considering this they should also have regard to the guidance on day care and educational services for under fives and that on day care services for school age children which give advice on quality and the proportion of qualified staff in each type of day care setting.

Advice

3.36. Local authorities should ensure that people working with families with children in need, in whatever setting and under whatever arrangements have been made to provide services in support, know where to turn for advice. People working in day care settings or as childminders should also know where to turn for advice. This does not mean that local authorities have to be the source of advice. But it should be recognised that people working with children may sometimes feel isolated and stressed. Ready access to advice helps them provide good quality services. Local authorities should also have regard to their duty under paragraph 8 of Schedule 2 to make available advice for children in need. This also applies to guidance and counselling services.

Guidance

3.37.   Local authorities should have an agreed policy on the need to issue detailed guidance about services and their delivery. Where this is done it should be within the framework of this guidance.

Counselling

3.38.   People looking after or working with children may find the task stressful and frustrating at times. This can lead to feelings of inadequacy and ultimately inability to provide services to an acceptable standard. Local authorities should have an agreed policy about the provision of counselling for parents, those with parental responsibility or looking after a child and workers, and should ensure that information about this is available. It need not be provided by the local authority but all concerned should know how to gain access to the service.

Family Aides

3.39.   This term describes the service under which the local authority provides someone to live in the family home for a short spell or to go daily, usually to help with the task of running the household. This can be useful in cases of prolonged illness or to help parents cope with a child with disabilities. It is often this sort of practical help which is difficult to arrange when a family is facing a crisis and parents therefore value it.

Other Facilities

3.40.   Local authorities should consider what other support might be given to help them discharge their duties and assist parents and providers in bringing up or caring for children. Services might include use of rooms for meetings, access to bulk-buy opportunities or photocopying/printing services.

CHAPTER 4 DAY CARE: FUNCTIONS OF LOCAL AUTHORITIES AND DEVELOPMENT OF SERVICES

4.1. The Act gives local authorities these duties and powers to provide, regulate and (with local education authorities) review day care services in their area:

- local authorities have a general duty to provide day care services for children in need and in making such arrangements to have regard to the different racial groups in the area to which the children belong (section 18 and Schedule 2 paragraph 11);

- local authorities have a duty to regulate the private and voluntary day care sectors and childminders (Part X and Schedule 9);

- local authorities have a duty to publish information about services provided by themselves and others and to ensure that this information is received by those who might benefit from them (Schedule 2 para 1);

- social services departments and local education authorities have a duty jointly to conduct and publish a report on a review of day care provision used by under 8's in the area at least once every 3 years (section 19);

- local authorities have power to provide day care for children who are not in need (section 18 and Schedule 2 paragraph 11);

- local authorities have power to provide facilities such as training, advice, guidance and counselling for adults working in a day care setting (including as a childminder) and for parents, or those with parental responsibility or looking after children, who stay with a child attending day care (section 18).

4.2. Under the Education Act 1980 local education authorities have power to decide whether or not to provide nursery education for children aged under five in a maintained school or class.

4.3. These legislative provisions give the social services and education departments of local authorities jointly and separately three functions:

- an oversight and co-ordinator function in conducting and publishing a report on the review of day care services;

- providing and managing their own services;

- regulating the private and voluntary day care sector and childminding (social services departments only).

The exercise of these roles should involve other departments within the local authority. In the case of Metropolitan Districts and London Boroughs these are:

- legal
- planning
- fire
- police
- environmental health
- recreation and leisure
- libraries
- health and safety
- housing
- economic development.

In the case of County Councils, planning, housing, environmental health, leisure and libraries are the responsibility of the district councils.

4.4. Local authorities, acting as corporate bodies, should decide on the mechanism for ensuring that all the relevant departments contribute actively to policy development on services for young children. In so doing they must have regard to the legislation governing referral or delegation of functions to committees.

4.5. A local authority may in relation to general services refer or delegate a matter to a separate committee of the council. For example, under the provisions of the Local Authority Social Services Act 1970 policy on general services for young children might be referred by the council to a committee other than the Social Services Committee to which functions specified in the Schedule to the 1970 Act must otherwise stand referred. Whenever a local authority does this, it must first consider a report from the Social Services Committee. Legislation governing social services and education requires the local authority to set up both Social Services and Education Committees. These carry out specific functions which, not relating to general services, cannot be referred or delegated to another committee. In the case of the Social Services Committee, for example, registration under the Children Act is not a general matter and so cannot stand referred to any other committee. A local authority may delegate functions relating to education to the Education Committee but not to another committee. A local authority may arrange for the discharge of functions by an officer in certain circumstances (section 101 of the Local Government Act 1972).

4.6. Local authorities may adopt a variety of strategies for transferring responsibilities to a joint committee or sub-committee, while maintaining the accountability of the Social Services or Education Committees for discharge of particular functions required under the legislation. Such an approach would facilitate the development of a framework for planning, managing and implementing a co-ordinated policy. Local authorities which have adopted positive policies towards services for young children have used different routes to develop a co-ordinated approach and have set up a variety of structures. Different models will operate to best effect in different places: there is no ideal model. Local authorities should work out the most efficient structure in the light of their own circumstances. (Annex B gives some examples of committee structure, officer support and advisory groups).

THE OVERSIGHT AND CO-ORDINATION FUNCTION

4.7. The legislation, which covers service provision, regulation of other services and review of the whole, provides the necessary statutory force for the effective exercise of the above function by local authorities and local education authorities. Over many years, a range and variety of day care, educational and family support services has been developed which has created choice for many parents. But the coherent and efficient use of services and the establishment of new ones needs to be subject to oversight by local authorities. In developing this function local authorities should have regard to these points:

- the mechanism for developing policy and its implementation;
- use of information obtained in the exercise of statutory functions (for example registration of private and voluntary day care);
- arrangements for identifying gaps in services;
- positive encouragement of development of services in the independent sector;
- links with other departments and other statutory authorities – for example health authorities and NHS Trusts;
- links with local voluntary organisations, community groups, ethnic minority interests, private childcare sector, employer interests – public sector, private sector and commercial;
- mechanisms for establishing links with voluntary and private sectors and employer interests.

THE PROVIDER FUNCTION

4.8. Local authorities should decide whether they wish to exercise the power in section 18(2) and (5) to provide day care for children who are not in need. It is unlikely, in view of other requirements under the Act, that public funds will be sufficient to provide day care for all parents who wish to use such a service. However, the social services department of a local authority, in consultation with other departments and interests, may decide it is appropriate in certain circumstances to set up a day care service in their area for a wide range of children. For instance:

- in an area of multiple disadvantage where there was concern for the welfare of families generally;

- where there is a need to upgrade a locality in order to attract investment, employment and training;

- as a means of pump-priming to encourage other organisations to set up facilities.

Such a service could consist of a combination of services directly provided and services sponsored or contracted for in independent facilities.

THE REGULATORY FUNCTION

4.9. The introduction of a modernised registration system provides local authorities with an opportunity to look critically at the way in which they exercise their regulatory function. The main purposes of registration are:

- to protect children;

- to provide reassurance to persons using independent services who are arranging for their child to be looked after by someone who is not a relation and may be a stranger;

- to ensure that services meet acceptable standards;

- to ensure that people wishing to provide services for children do so within an agreed framework.

Any applicant for registration is planning to provide a service for young children for which he may charge. This applies to voluntary organisations, community groups, childminders, employers and the private sector. It follows that registration has to be a positive process, there to help the setting up of good quality services for families to use on an informed basis and with confidence. Applications must be handled promptly and sympathetically.

4.10. Local authorities should therefore use this function in an enabling and facilitating way and seek to encourage developments. They have a wealth of knowledge and expertise about day care services for young children and how to provide and maintain acceptable standards of care. This should be shared with intending providers and childminders so that there is a clear understanding about the standards required and the reasons for them. Local authorities should also recognise the expertise or knowledge which may be held by those applying for registration and work to build on this.

BRINGING THE FUNCTIONS TOGETHER

4.11. Whilst the oversight and co-ordinator, the provider, and the regulatory roles have distinct features, which demand different skills, they need to be carried out in co-operation. Social services and education departments within a local authority cannot carry out the review duty effectively without seeking information from the registration staff about their work and from the people responsible for the management of the authority's own day care and educational provision for children below statutory school age. Day care services should be of comparable quality, whether they are managed by social services departments of local authorities themselves or an independent provider; this involves exchange of information and opportunities for discussion and learning about different ways of working and delivery of services.

4.12. Local authorities are well placed to ensure that all services for young children are efficiently and effectively organised and delivered to acceptable standards. It is important that their approach to this work is one which enables the participation of all interested organisations.

DEVELOPMENT OF SERVICES

4.13. In each area there will be a wide range of providers involved in developing and running day care services – different departments in local authorities, other statutory bodies, voluntary organisations, self-help or community groups. volunteers, private companies, private individuals running a business or working as a childminder or nanny, and employers in the public and private sectors. The pattern, level and delivery of services should be worked out locally and the process should involve all interested parties who include those mentioned above and community interests, ethnic minority groups and parents, churches and other places of worship. The new review duty provides a useful framework within which to develop services.

Role of the Private Sector

4.14. In recent years the private day care sector has expanded considerably and increased choice for parents. This sector has much to contribute to the range and pattern of services in each area and local authorities should ensure that private day care providers are fully involved in, and consulted about any changes and developments in policy and practice. Attention should also be paid to the scope for partnership. Local authorities should inform themselves about the private day care sector in their area so that they can play a full part in discussions and proper account may be taken of the services this sector provides.

Role of Voluntary Organisations

4.15. Over the years many voluntary organisations have developed considerable knowledge and expertise about services for young children and their families and how these support parents. They involve the community in a variety of ways in their activities and services and their presence in an area can help to improve the quality of provision. Voluntary organisations may also be able to respond to requests or demands for new and additional services, particularly in an emergency, and they are a source of innovatory or unusual ideas for delivery of services and ways of enhancing children's development. It is important that local authorities have a detailed knowledge of local voluntary organisations in their area and their strengths so that they work with them in partnership both in the field of day care and more generally.

Role of the Volunteer

4.16. Local authorities should recognise the importance of the volunteer in the field of day care. The playgroup movement and befriending services for families under stress (such as Home-Start schemes) are examples of using volunteers to provide services for families with young children. It should be recognised that volunteers may need help, support and training in order to be effective. Both examples given above have developed effective networks within their own organisations to support volunteers but in some cases it may not be locally based and may be poorly resourced. Local authorities should have regard to the recruitment of volunteers and ensure that as far as possible the racial mix within an area is properly reflected. They should also ensure that there are well publicised means of providing the appropriate support. This does not mean that staff in social services departments should undertake to do either task themselves but they need to ensure that both are done. This could involve grant aid to a local organisation or offering places on training courses or a telephone advice or help line.

Links Between Day Care Providers and Childminding

4.17. There should be close links between the different forms of day care in an area – for example between day nurseries, playgroups, out of school clubs and childminding – because this will be mutually supportive. A group of childminders might be attached formally or informally to a day nursery and visit it regularly with the children they care for. A day care provider might wish to operate with a network of childminders linked to the day nursery in order to offer a very flexible service to parents and children. This type of flexible service further increases choice for parents and can be a valuable resource for the whole community.

CHAPTER 5   NEED FOR SERVICES AND INFORMATION

5.1. This chapter outlines children's need for services including play , parents' need for day care and the role of information services.

CHILDREN'S NEED FOR SERVICES

Under Fives

5.2. By the time they reach the age of five, the great majority of children will have been to a group day care facility or a nursery or primary class. Some children will have attended a facility part- time and some full-time with some going to more than one type of facility in a week. Up to 10% of children will not have attended any such facility before starting full-time school at the age of five. (See paragraph 37 of **Starting with Quality – the Report of the Committee of Inquiry into the Quality of Educational Experience Offered to 3 and 4 Year Olds chaired by Mrs Angela Rumbold CBE MP (HMSO 1990)** – referred to as the Rumbold Report).

5.3. Children benefit in terms of their social, emotional, intellectual and physical development from spending some time with their peers and adults who are not part of the immediate family. Up to the age of three children may enjoy being with other children but are less likely to play as a group, preferring to play on their own or with one adult. From the age of about three most children will have begun to understand about sharing toys and taking turns and their confidence, maturity and independence are likely to be enhanced by being with their peers.

Children of Statutory School Age

5.4. There is little statistical information about how school age children use their leisure time or the quantity of services available whose primary purpose is to look after them while parents are at work, following higher education or training courses or otherwise not available outside the school day and in the holidays. It is thought that among children of primary school age about 20% return to an empty house – so-called 'latchkey children'. The percentage is likely to be higher among children of secondary school age. In most parts of the country there is a rich variety of activities and pastimes for school age children but there are very few out-of-school clubs or holiday schemes offering care while parents are not available. While most school age children do not attend a general out of school facility, many are likely to take part in some form of organised activity with their peers for a few hours each week.

5.5. Research evidence is not conclusive about the benefits in terms of children's all round development of attending a day care service or supervised activity which provides opportunities for school age children to be with their peers and take part in group activities. Many consider that school age children need opportunities to take part in activities where they are responsible for choosing what to do, for the setting up of the project or task and its completion in order to develop self-confidence, foster skills, and build individual and group relationships. It is also thought that the way in which children use non-school time and the quality of their out of school experience affects their later development and ultimately full enjoyment of adult life.

PLAY

5.6. Children's need for good quality play opportunities changes as they grow up, but they need such opportunities throughout childhood in order to reach and maintain their optimum development and well- being. Under fives develop knowledge of themselves and their world through play – see the advice on play in paragraphs 89 to 91 of the Rumbold Report. For school age children play is a means whereby they can develop a broader range of interests, complementary to subjects learnt during school time, and a positive approach to use of leisure time.

5.7. Local authority staff working in the day care field as policy makers, advisers, managers or registration or inspection officers should develop understanding about the role of play in terms of child development. Staff in the leisure or recreation departments are likely to have knowledge and expertise on this aspect.

PARENTS' NEED FOR DAY CARE

5.8. 41% of women with dependent children aged under five are in paid employment – 12% full time and 29% part time – and the percentage rises to 66% – 20% full time, 46% part time – for women with children of primary school age and 74% – 31% full time and 43% part time – for women with children of secondary school age. 17% of families with dependent children are headed by a single parent, usually the mother. Thus many children are likely to experience some form of non-parental care from a young age.

5.9. It is for parents or those with parental responsibility to decide in the light of their own circumstances whether to take up paid employment outside the home while their children are young. A child's development will depend on the quality of substitute care provided if parents are absent from the home during the day. There has been much debate about the most suitable form of non-parental care for babies and toddlers (under twos) and whether a group setting is harmful. The research evidence available* suggests that the quality and consistency of the substitute care provided is crucial to the child's well-being.

5.10. It is for the parent or person with parental responsibility to decide who to entrust with the care of the children and to make the necessary arrangements for them to go to the facility. It is unreasonable to expect children aged under 8 to be wholly responsible for themselves and parents will have to make arrangements for someone else to look after them when or if they are unable to do so. For children aged over 8 it is generally accepted that parents, while encouraging a child's growing independence, need to ensure that their children are not exposed to risk of harm or injury. Section 3(5) of the Act makes clear that any person caring for a child, but not holding parental responsibility, may do what is reasonable in all the circumstances for the purposes of safeguarding or providing for the child's welfare. This would allow a carer to exercise delegated responsibility in the absence of the parent and take action in an emergency to protect the child. This should be the subject of a clear agreement between the parent and carer. In some circumstances – for example where the parents are not available for long periods of time – it will be necessary to make similar arrangements for older children to be looked after. In other circumstances older children may be capable of looking after themselves – by taking themselves to and from school and going to out of school activity such as a special club.

INFORMATION SERVICES

5.11. Section 19 and paragraph 1 of Schedule 2 to the Act require local authorities to publish information about the services they provide themselves and, where appropriate, those provided by other organisations. Parents currently find out about the different day care and related services available in their community from a variety of sources such as the health visitor, family doctor, relatives, neighbours, social services departments, health clinic, library,

---

*See **H Rudolph Schaffer Making Decisions about Children Psychological Questions and Answers (Basic Blackwell Oxford 1990).**

teachers, schools and friends of their children. In some areas local authorities or local voluntary groups produce a directory. In the last few years one or two independent information services based on the resource and referral centres found in the USA have been set up, where parents, carers, providers and employers can ask about the range of services available in a locality and the type of service provided and talk over their particular needs with skilled staff. Such services may help to identify gaps in provision and ways of filling them.

5.12. Policy makers, those responsible for the day to day running of services and people working in day care settings or with families experiencing difficulties should pay attention to how parents obtain information and, where appropriate, the use they make of it. Within each local authority there should be an agreed policy on information services for children and their families. It is important that the local authority as a whole is involved in this because much of the information may be dispersed between departments. The authority may wish to run such a service itself. There may be advantages in enabling an outside organisation to set up and run such a service because parents may find it more accessible. An attractive model, pioneered in the USA, is one which is managed on a partnership basis involving local voluntary bodies, employers, the private day care sector and the local authority.

CHAPTER 6 STANDARDS IN DAY CARE SERVICES FOR UNDER EIGHTS AND EDUCATIONAL PROVISION FOR UNDER FIVES

6.1. This chapter gives advice and guidance on the standards of provision which the Department consider acceptable in day care settings used by children aged under eight (including childminding). It also gives advice on the standards of provision in educational services for the under fives which the Department of Education and Science considers acceptable. These standards apply to all services – those managed by social services or education departments or other departments within a local authority and by independent providers and childminders. The chapter is divided into these 5 sections:

Section A   General Issues which apply across all settings and age groups

Section B   Quality of Care

Section C   Day care and educational services for under fives

Section D   Childminding

Section E   Day care services for school age children

SECTION A: GENERAL ISSUES

6.2. Certain general principles should inform good practice in day care, education and related services for young children and their families. These should include the following:

- children's welfare and development are paramount;
- children should be treated and respected as individuals whose needs (including special educational needs) should be catered for;
- parents' responsibility for their chidren should be recognised and respected;
- the values deriving from different backgrounds – racial, cultural, religious and linguistic – should be recognised and respected;
- parents are generally the first educators of their children; this should be reflected in the relationships with other carers and providers;
- parents should have easy access to information about services in their area and be able to make informed choices.

Programme of Activities

6.3. The day's programme should be planned before the facility opens or the children arrive. Different considerations apply depending on the opening hours of the facility, its primary purpose and the ages and numbers of children attending, but the main points to bear in mind are:

- the activities should be appropriate to age and developmental stage;
- there should be variety so that children are given opportunities to develop physical, cognitive and social skills;
- staff should involve the children in the planning of the activities;
- the programme should be flexible and should allow for quiet and noisy activities;
- in the case of children in a full day care setting there should be sufficient time for rests/naps;
- children should work at their own pace as much as possible.

6.4. As working with young children is demanding and complex, caregivers require a wide range of skills in order to provide good quality services. Training produces benefits for a variety of reasons. A trained person will understand how to respond sensitively to young children's needs. Parents are usually good at such responsiveness without any special training, but, because of the difference in their emotional commitment, such responsiveness may not be so automatic for caregivers. To some degree sensitive responsiveness will reflect personality characteristics but appropriate training will help to improve it for most care givers. Training can make caregivers more aware of stages in children's development and the need to adjust to the child's changing developmental needs. Caregiver training has also been associated with more competent peer interaction – see Chapters 10 and 16 of the Rumbold Report.

6.5. There are currently many different training courses available for people wishing to work in this field with some courses leading to a qualification – for example the certificate awarded by National Nursery Examination Board or the diploma awarded by the Business and Technician Education Council (BTEC) – and others offering a certificate of attendance but no indication about the level or range of skills obtained. The introduction of a system of National Vocational Qualifications will lead to nationally agreed standards across professions including day care for young children which will provide a framework within which it will be possible to assess levels of skill and competence. As National Vocational Qualifications enable people to acquire qualifications through assessment of work based learning as well as recognition of courses attended, it will be possible for more people working with young children to obtain qualifications. The documents produced by the Care Sector Consortium's Working with Under Sevens Project provide a useful framework for analysing the different tasks undertaken by workers. At the moment it is not possible to give detailed advice on the NVQ levels of competence to be held by people wishing to work as officers in charge of a full day care service, as deputies, as playgroup workers or other staff or as childminders. Local authorities should become familiar with the documents produced by the Working with Under Sevens project which have been endorsed by the Care Sector Consortium and use them as the basis for deciding about the level of qualifications needed for particular services.

6.6. People working with school age children in day care settings also need particular skills, and training provides a means of developing these. It is suggested that local authorities should inform themselves about training for playworkers which is being developed through the National Children's Play and Recreation Unit under the auspices of the Sport and Leisure Industry Lead Body and the National Council for Vocational Qualifications.

6.7. Many workers who already hold qualifications in day care or a related area will benefit from in-service or refresher training events and courses. These might be on specific topics, such as child protection or working with children with special educational needs, or on general issues such as child development. Multi-disciplinary training events or those which involve people working in different types of settings run by different organisations also provide an effective way of improving understanding of different skills. Local authorities should develop policy on training for their own day care staff and encourage independent providers to do this. It should underpin the exercise of their duties in respect of children in need and registration of independent providers and childminders. It is desirable that childminders are encouraged to take up training opportunities.

Special Educational Needs

6.8. Local authorities should have regard to the advice and guidance in Assessments and Statements of Special Educational Needs: procedures within the Education Health and Social Services (DES: 22/89, Annex to HN(89)20, HN(FP)(89)19 and LASSL (89)7) and to the volume **Services for Children with**

Disabilities in this series which is issued separately. Generally the development of young children with disabilities or special educational needs is more likely to be enhanced through attending a day care service for under eights or educational service for under fives used by all children. Policy workers, registration officers, providers and practitioners need to consider the means whereby this aim might be achieved in discussion with experts in the field such as health professionals and people working for relevant voluntary organisations. In making arrangements for integrating children with disabilities with other children in a day care or pre- school education setting, particular attention should be paid to the physical environment, staff/child ratios, and training (eg in sign language for the profoundly deaf). It may also be desirable for there to be services catering specifically for children with disabilities and special educational needs but these might, with advantage, be attached to a service used by all children so that joint activities can be arranged from time to time.

Equal Opportunties and Racial Groups

6.9. The Act requires local authorities (Schedule 2 paragraph 11) in making arrangements for provision of day care, to 'have regard to the different racial groups to which children within their area who are in need belong' and in the exercise of their power to cancel someone's registration on the grounds of seriously inadequate care to have regard to the child's 'religious persuasion, racial origin and cultural and linguistic background'. (section 74(1)(b)(2)(b) and (6)). The Race Relations Act 1976 gives local authorities a duty to promote good race relations.

6.10. People working with young children should value and respect the different racial origins, religions, cultures and languages in a multi-racial society so that each child is valued as an individual without racial or gender stereotyping. Children from a very young age learn about different races and cultures including religion and languages and will be capable of assigning different values to them. The same applies to gender and making distinctions between male and female roles. It is important that people working with young children are aware of this, so that their practice enables the children to develop positive attitudes to differences of race, culture and language and differences of gender.

6.11. Local authorities should have approved equal opportunities policies including arrangements for monitoring and reviewing progress towards implementation. They should ensure that they have available data on the ethnic origins of the local population which is essential for assessment of the extent to which the day care and educational services for the under fives in the area are operating in a non-discriminatory way. Local authorities should also ensure that the arrangements for involving independent organisations and individuals in the exercise of the review duty enable all racial groups within the area to contribute fully. This may involve providing interpreter and translation services as well as seeing that arrangements for consultative meetings and their membership do not discriminate.

Parental Involvement

6.12. Local authorities need to ensure that their policies on day care for under eights, provision of education for the under fives and the exercise of their duties and powers under the Act properly reflect the importance of involving parents. Those concerned must recognise that parents generally have the greatest knowledge of their own child. Parents should be kept fully informed about their child's activities in a day care or educational setting or with a childminder. Providers should make sure that there are sufficient opportunities for parents and the people who work with the child to discuss his progress and plans for future activities. In the case of childminders the relationship with the parents is likely to be close and there are daily opportunities to exchange information about activities and progress. The same principles apply, although it may be necessary to make special arrangements to discuss progress when the childminder and the parents are not having to respond to the demands of children.

6.13. In the case of day care or educational facilities in non domestic premises, there will be a variety of management arrangements with some being managed by a statutory body, some by a commercial company or individual as a business, some by a voluntary body and some by a committee, possibly on a self-help basis. Whatever the arrangements are, there should be an agreed policy on parental involvement. The policy should ensure that, as well as having time to talk about their child's activities, parents are also able to express their views on management issues and are fully consulted about changes. In some cases – for example playgroups and community day nurseries – parents are actively involved in managing the service and some may work as unpaid volunteers with the children. In others there may be a user committee to act as a forum for discussion and consultation. In a facility such as a playgroup where there is a philosophy of parental involvement in all aspects – management, organisation and day to day operation – those responsible should make sure that parents who are unable, for whatever reason, to give much time to the work of the playgroup are nevertheless able to make a contribution in another way. (See also paragraph 99 of the Rumbold Report).

Health Issues

6.14. Organisations and individuals responsible for running or working in day care services should establish effective working relationships with health authorities in their area at an appropriate level so that there are agreed arrangements for obtaining advice from health professionals on matters relating to the health and development of children and also in an emergency. The Department commends the practice in some day nurseries having a named doctor and health visitor from whom they may seek advice.

6.15. Where a day care provider or childminder identifies a possible need for specialist help for a child – eg speech therapy, physiotherapy – he must tell the parents so that they may take the appropriate steps to obtain advice and if necessary treatment for the child. In no circumstances should a provider or childminder take such action on their own initiative.

6.16. A child needs to be in optimum health in order to benefit from his day care or educational experience. Children aged under five, who are in a day nursery or with a childminder, should not miss out on the child health surveillance programme. *Health checks are usually offered at age 6 weeks, 8 months (range 7 to 9 months), 21 months (range 18 to 24 months), 39 months (range 36 to 42 months) and on school entry at 5 years (range 48 to 66 months). Providers and childminders should make sure that they are informed by the parents about their child's health checks. Where appropriate providers and childminders should remind parents about the checks and the ages at which they are due. In areas where parents hold the child's health record* providers and childminders should encourage the parents to show it to them.

6.17. In all day care facilities there should be at least one member of staff with first aid training who is responsible for keeping the first aid box fully supplied and checking its contents from time to time. Managers should ensure that all staff have a working knowledge of first aid. Childminders should also have at least a working knowledge of first aid and first aid box whose contents are checked regularly. It is recommended that childminders are encouraged to undergo first aid training. Local branches of the Red Cross or St. John Ambulance are useful sources of advice and training.

6.18. Food hygiene and the arrangements for safe storage and preparation of snacks and meals are important for ensuring that children do not become unwell whilst in day care or with a childminder. There are booklets on Food Safety (published in the Food Sense series) and the Food Handlers Guide (HMSO 1990) which give advice on this issue for the general public and people working

---

*Health for All Children: A Programme of Child Health Surveillance edited DMB Hall.

in the catering industry as cooks or food handlers. These provide useful basic information on this topic.

Staffing

6.19. The staff/child ratios in this chapter are those that will normally be needed to secure good quality care or education for young children. Local authorities should use them in deciding what requirements should be observed by people providing day care for the under eights and by childminders. Factors to be taken into account include:

- the opening hours of the different services;
- the need for staff to spend most of their working day in direct contact with the children;
- the particular need for very young children to receive some one-to-one attention;
- qualifications, training and experience of the staff;
- the overall size of the facility;
- the stage of development reached by particular children e.g. the presence of children with disabilities.

6.20. The ratios recommended are derived from judgements of how to put into practice the general objectives quality of care in paragraph 6.25. Local authorities should base their requirements in respect of each application for registration on an *overall* assessment of the quality and standards of the particular facility.

Behaviour and Sanctions

6.21. People responsible for running a day care facility need to have an agreed policy on its day to day operation and to develop procedures for modifying unacceptable behaviour in the children which will include appropriate sanctions. It will encourage development of a sense of right and wrong behaviour if children are encouraged to co-operate in the social organisation of the facility. The sanctions applied in the case of unacceptable behaviour must take account of the age and stage of development of the child, be given at the time, be relevant to the action or actions and be fair. The child should always be told why his behaviour is not acceptable and the reasons for applying a particular sanction. Providers and childminders should ensure that parents are fully informed about and support the policy on modifying unacceptable behaviour and the range of sanctions.

6.22. Corporal punishment (smacking, slapping or shaking) is illegal in maintained schools and should not be used by any other parties within the scope of this guidance. It is permissible to take necessary physical action in an emergency to prevent personal injury either to the child, other children or an adult or serious damage to property.

Public Liability Insurance

6.23. It is good practice for day care providers and childminders to carry public liability insurance. Parents need to be reassured that the service or person who has undertaken to care for their child is paying due attention to the business side of the arrangement. Evidence of up-to-date and adequate public liability insurance cover is a good way to demonstrate this. Local authorities should encourage day care providers and childminders to take out such insurance cover.

SECTION B: QUALITY OF CARE

6.24. Quality of care is influenced by complex factors, and those responsible for services for young children within local authorities should develop their knowledge and understanding of the issue, so that there is general agreement about aims and objectives. It is desirable that all concerned with services for young children inform themselves about and keep up to date with research in this field. The Bibliography lists a selection of current literature on day care which covers quality as well as other issues.

6.25. The main factors which influence quality of care are:

- the nature of adult/child interaction;
- the nature of the interaction between children/peers;
- size of group and numbers of staff;
- continuity, training and experience of staff;
- recognition of children's developmental needs;
- type of contract/involvement between parent and provider;
- ability to structure and support children's learning;
- elements in programme of activities;
- equality of opportunity policy in employment and service delivery;
- children's involvement in planning and choosing activities and projects;
- elements of imagination, challenge and adventure in activities;
- organisation, display and accessibility of equipment, toys and materials;
- attention to health, safety and type of physical environment.

6.26. Defining quality of care involves looking at these factors from the point of view of child development as well as the rights or expectations of children, parents and people working with young children.

Child Development

6.27. This involves focusing on the child's experience in terms of the potential advantages and disadvantages that the experience offers the child and the possible effects of the care upon child development. One aspect of good quality care is that it is developmentally beneficial to the child, and poor quality care is that which inhibits, or at least does not facilitate, child development. Most research on quality has been explicitly or implicitly guided by this approach.

Rights or Expectations of Children

6.28. Children have a right to an environment which facilitates their development. An approach based on children's rights would encompass all the factors necessary for their development. However, depending upon the values held by society at large, the child may be regarded as having rights which go beyond the provision of an environment which can be empirically demonstrated to facilitate development. For example: children should have the right to be cared for as part of a community which values the religious, racial, cultural and linguistic identity of the child. The justification for the awarding of such a right would be in terms of fostering the child's sense of identity. Children's sense of identity is a fundamental aspect of their development and so such a right could be included within a definition based upon the facilitation of child development. Other examples of rights which might be assigned to children include the right to health, individuality, respect, dignity, oportunities for learning and socializing with adults and children, freedom from discrimination such as racism or sexism and cultural diversity. The extent to which a day care setting fulfils these rights may be used in defining the quality of care for that setting. All these rights can be regarded as potentially contributing to children's physical, intellectual, social and emotional development. There is research evidence which specifies the details of the relationship between the experience of the rights and subsequent development. For example the right to a stable learning and caring environment can be specified in terms of which aspects of that environment will facilitate which aspects of intellectual, linguistic or social development. Assumptions about the appropriate childcare practices in relation to some other rights – the right to cultural diversity for example – have yet to be tested by research.

Rights or Expectations of Parents

6.29. The two approaches outlined above are child-centred. However certain parental rights should be considered as part of a definition of quality of care because this enables parents to influence the nature of their children's care environments. To this end the following opportunities for parents should be considered:

- to acquire information about the care environment;
- to express their views on the care environment;
- to alter the care environment of their child;
- to contribute to their child's care environment;
- to choose between alternative childcare environments.

This approach enables parents to have some choice over division of their time between parenting and other activities. Access to services, choice between services, transport to services and hours during which care is available, are all relevant for parents wishing to make informed choices.

Rights or Expectations of People Working with Young Children

6.30. The characteristics of the care environment will be dramatically influenced by the characteristics of the workers, and the workers themselves will be affected by the environments in which they work. There are therefore good grounds for including the rights of workers in a consideration of the quality of care. The research evidence linking staffing characteristics and children's experience and development is considered below. Another approach is to consider the rights of the worker as an employee and the extent to which employment rights are met within a particular setting. While there are differences between these approaches, they overlap in so far as conditions of services for workers can be shown to influence the nature of children's experience in ways which have implications for their development.

Research Evidence and the Quality of Care

6.31. Quality of care is defined in terms of experiences which affect children's development and well-being. Research on child development points to several aspects of the young child's experience as having potential developmental consequences including adult-child interaction, peer interaction, interpersonal relationships, learning opportunities, health and safety and whether children are happy.

Adult — Child Interaction

6.32. There are several studies in home and day care settings which reveal positive developmental benefits associated with aspects of adult-infant interaction, notably affection and sensitive responsiveness between adult and child. Children enrolled in day care with more responsive caregivers are likely to have better cognitive and language development and also to be more socially competent. Research in home environments has also found that responsive interaction fosters secure attachments and it seems likely that similar processes will operate in day care settings.

Peer Interaction

6.33. Where children have more experience of peer interaction their skills in such interaction improve, and this can be an advantage for children receiving out-of-home care. One of the great benefits of the expansion of group day care services since the early 1960's – for example the growth in the number of playgroups – has been the increased opportunities for under fives to develop their skills in peer interaction. This has become more important with the general reduction in family size, increased mobility of families and other factors which have led to greater isolation of families with young children and a consequent reduction in other opportunities for peer play for under fives. There is ample evidence that the social skills of three to five year old children are facilitated by group experience in a variety of sessional and full day care settings. Same-age and mixed-age groups including children with learning difficulties supply useful and complementary forms of experience, and if children can experience both sorts of group that will probably be beneficial.

Interpersonal Relationships

6.34. Secure attachment relationships are associated with a wide range of developmental advantages for the child. Where a warm secure relationship exists between adult and child, the child is better able to use the adult to explore the environment. This is true in the home, and in day care where children are securely attached to a caregiver. Toddlers show different patterns of social interaction with stable caregivers. Such differences may well account for the developmental effects sometimes associated with instability of care. Young children learning to communicate will often use idiosyncratic speech or gestures and a caregiver who is familiar with a child is most likely to know such idiosyncracies, and be able to respond quickly and appropriately, than a new caregiver. Research such as the **American National Day Care Staffing Study** demonstrates the importance of stability of caregivers and finds poorer language and social development associated with higher staff turnover. There are two major aspects involved in stability of care. One concerns the continuity of the care placements, and the other the stability of caregivers within a placement. In both cases the greater the instability the more detrimental it will be for the child's experience. It is very likely that stability may be more important in the case of younger children at a period when the establishment of stable interpersonal relationships and the development of communications skills are more vulnerable. In peer relationships social and sophisticated role playing proceeds better between good friends, so that stable peer groups are more likely to foster competent social skills. Stability of care is likely therefore to be strongly associated with the nature of the interpersonal relationships which a child forms with adults and peers with possible consequences for the child's development.

Learning Opportunities

6.35. Young children are continuously learning about the environment and people around them. The way in which experiences are structured affect how learning progresses. People working with young children should be skilled in structuring and supporting that learning. Sometimes learning opportunities are explicitly planned for, but often they are inherent in the daily activities of the children. Children will obviously benefit in terms of communicative and cognitive competence more from environments which provide the most appropriate learning opportunities. Indeed, they are likely to become bored and even upset in situations which are unstimulating. Children need variety in their experience and their activities need to be adapted to their developmental level to provide good learning opportunities. Three to five year olds in day care settings can benefit when there is input from people trained in education in the early years. With the advent of the National Curriculum, workers should know in particular what activities enable children to develop understanding and knowledge of the concepts included in the curriculum as they approach the age of five.

Health and Safety Conditions

6.36. The importance of health and safety is obvious. A child who is made sick or injured by its surroundings is not benefiting from them. A hazardous environment may also distract caregivers from optimising the experiences of children and force them to control the children in such a way as to limit exploration which is a basic mechanism of learning.

6.37. If the above aspects of experience are catered for children will generally be happy and contented and there is evidence of the positive effects this has on development. The learning of new concepts, for example, proceeds more efficiently when children are happy. Unhappy children do not explore their environments and will often cut themselves off from the outside world. Communication proceeds more effectively when children are in a happy state of mind, and so the benefits of all kinds of interaction are likely to be increased when the emotional climate is favourable.

6.38. Together, these aspects of a child's experience in a care environment constitute a definition of the quality of care. This is not the only possible definition, but it is derived from explicit assumptions and demonstrable empirical evidence. In this approach the quality of care is examined under separate headings which can be measured. As more empirical evidence becomes available these may be expanded to take account of new perspectives. Deciding whether services run by day care providers or offered by individuals (childminders) are of acceptable quality involves a value judgement. There should be a clear understanding about the value base and the criteria used for assessing the quality of care in these situations.

SECTION C: STANDARDS FOR DAY CARE AND EDUCATIONAL SERVICES FOR UNDER FIVES

6.39. This section gives guidance on the space standards and overall size, staff/child ratios, group size within the facility, furnishing and equipment and observation and records under these headings:

- full day care
- sessional day care
- maintained nursery schools and classes
- combined centres
- private nursery schools.

Annex C gives brief descriptions of the different types of service used by children aged under five.

Education in Day Care Settings

6.40. The aim should be to offer 3 and 4 year olds in day care settings experiences comparable in quality with those offered to children attending school. What children experience at these ages is crucial for their confidence and competence when embarking on their compulsory schooling. It is for policy makers, providers and practitioners to decide how this aim is to be met. The part time services of teachers trained to deal with the early years may be a valuable resource in a day nursery. Social services departments within a local authority should ensure that this point is considered in the development of their day care policies. In so doing they should have regard to the powers contained in the Act (for example section 27 in Part III, and Schedule 9 paragraph 8) to seek advice and help from education departments. Section 26 of the Education Act 1980 gives local education authorities power to deploy early years trained teachers to work in day nurseries.

Full Day Care

6.41. The term includes 'extended day playgroups' and 'creches' in shopping centres, training establishments, leisure facilities or equivalent as well as day nurseries run by statutory authorities, voluntary bodies, private companies or community groups.

(a) Staff/Child Ratios

The standard recommended ratios are:

0 to 2 years = 1:3
2 to 3 years = 1:4
3 to 5 years = 1:8

Managers or officers in charge should be treated as supernumerary when considering the ratios where the service has places for more than 20 children because most of their time will be taken up with administration and the management of staff. A higher ratio may be appropriate for the following reasons: if not all the staff are qualified or sufficiently trained; if there are very young babies (under 12 months) who need constant attention. Officers in charge and their deputies should hold a relevant qualification in either child care, early years education, social work, health visiting or children's nursing. They should also have experience of working with young children. At least half the staff should also be qualified in child care, early years education or social work and other staff should be encouraged to follow relevant training courses. Each facility should have adequate support staff – for example cooks, cleaners, clerical staff – so that those employed to care for the children are not required to prepare food, carry out other domestic tasks, undertake routine administration or be involved in maintenance of the premises or equipment.

(b) Premises and Space Standards

Day nurseries may be found in purpose built or converted buildings. Whatever type of building is used, the environment should be warm, welcoming, light and make the children feel at home. These space standards which represent clear space per child are desirable:

Age of child	Square Feet	Square Metres
0 to 2 years	40	3.7
2 to 3 years	30	2.8
3 to 5 years	25	2.3

Fixtures such as cupboards should be excluded when considering whether there is adequate space. As the premises used for day nurseries are very different, the way in which the space can be used will vary.

These points should be taken into account:

- no room (regardless of size) should have to accommodate more than 26 children except for special occasions and, where possible, the maximum should be lower for younger children;

- there should be a separate room for babies and toddlers with proper facilities for nappy changing and preparation of feeds close to it;

- there should be separate areas or, where possible, rooms for quiet, noisy and messy activities;

- there should be appropriate facilities for children with disabilities;

- there should be a minimum of 1 lavatory to 10 children with the same number of wash hand basins;

- there must be separate toilet facilities for staff;

- there should be office space and a staff room;

- there must be a kitchen which should be of an appropriate size and adequately equipped to provide meals and snacks for children and staff; it should conform to environmental health and food safety regulations;

- there should be outside play space, preferably adjacent to the building and exclusively for the use of the children. Where this is not achievable – for example in an urban area – proper arrangements must be made so that the children are taken regularly to local parks or playgrounds or the equivalent.

If possible there should be space for parents or other local groups to meet. The person in charge will wish to have a room where he talks to parents or other individuals.

(c) Maximum Number of Places

Where it is proposed to set up a day nursery with more than 50 places, the premises and layout should be organised so that the children are accommodated in self-contained units of not more than 26. Facilities with less than 50 places should also be organised with this principle in mind but it may not be practicable or sensible to have completely self-contained units.

(d) Size of Groups within the Facility or Unit

Generally children do better in small groups rather than large groups. This is so for a wide range of developmental indicators. The size of group which is most beneficial will change with the age of the children. Babies and toddlers generally need smaller groups than older children. For three and four year olds research suggests an upper limit of 6-8 for peer group size to optimise peer interaction. Larger groups may lead to overstimulation and disruption. This also applies to sessional facilities.

(e) Furniture and Equipment

The furniture and equipment provided should help to create a warm, cheerful, stimulating and safe environment. Chairs and tables should be child-sized with enough small tables to allow children to choose between different activities and places. Where possible there should be low adult-sized seating so that staff can sit comfortably on a level with the children. Vinyl floor coverings should be non-slip but easy to clean. Carpeted areas help to identify places for different types of activity. There should be a wide range of equipment available, so that children can safely develop their social, cognitive, and physical skills. The equipment, which should reflect multi-racial society in a positive way, should include materials for art, craft, music, manipulative and construction activities, for exploring the natural world and developing physical skills. This also applies to sessional facilities.

(f) Toys

Facilities should have sufficient toys available to provide stimulating, safe and developmentally appropriate activities for the children. Providers need to have a clear policy on buying and replacing toys which is subject to regular review. In developing such a policy providers should, where appropriate, seek expert advice – for example from toy libraries. This also applies to sessional facilities.

(g) Snacks and Meals

Providers should ensure that the snacks and meals provided are varied and nutritious. Meals should be chosen to reflect the cultural and religious backgrounds of the children. Parents' wishes should be respected and as far as practicable taken account of in the meals and snacks provided. Meal and snack times should be treated as social occasions with staff eating with small groups of children.

(h) Observation and Records

The Act requires providers to keep records of the children attending a day care service. This requirement is confined to factual details about the child and his parents. It is also important that people working with young children in a full day care setting observe what each child within the facility is doing, assess what this means in terms of learning and development, report and record it. The advice in Chapter 7 of the Rumbold Report which explains clearly the benefits of this approach for children and emphasises the importance of sharing the information gathered with the parents.

Local authorities and providers should have regard to **Young Children in Group Day Care: Guidelines for Good Practice (National Children's Bureau** forthcoming).

6.42. This term covers facilities which are open for mornings or afternoons only where no main meals are provided. These facilities are mainly used by children aged from 3 to 5 rather than babies or toddlers, although some may admit children from the age of 2½.

(a) Staff/Child Ratios

The standard recommended ratio is 1.8 for children aged 3 to 5. This is based on the assumption that workers will not expect to have time for a break during the session and will be in direct contact with the children throughout. Some sessional facilities such as playgroups are likely to use volunteers on a regular basis to work with the children. Regular volunteers should be treated as part of the overall ratio. In all cases at least half of the staff should hold a relevant qualification in day care, or education, or have completed a training course specified by the Pre-School Playgroups Association (PPA) or other voluntary body.

(b) Premises and Space Standards

Sessional day care will be provided in a variety of premises. Many playgroups will share community centres, village or church halls with other users. Some rent rooms from schools where they are likely to have sole use of that space with (possibly) access to other facilities in the school. A few own their premises – often demountable buildings attached to a school or other institution. 25 square foot per child (2.3 square metres) of clear space is desirable. There should be a minimum of 1 lavatory per 10 children. It is desirable to have more than one room so that quiet and noisy activities can be separate and there is space for children to rest. Organisers should ensure access to outside playspace which should where possible be adjacent to the premises. This may not always be possible and organisers should make arrangements to take the children to playgrounds or local parks or equivalent from time to time.

(c) Snacks

All facilities should provide snacks and drinks for the children during the session. These should be varied, nutritious and chosen to reflect the cultural and religious backgrounds of the children attending.

(d) Observation and Records

The advice in 6.41(h) should be generally followed in the case of sessional facilities but perhaps in a less formal way. In particular there may be more emphasis on oral reporting to parents and other individuals rather than keeping written records.

6.43. Nursery education – whether in nursery schools or in nursery classes – is mainly offered on a part-time basis. However, attendance for the full school day is more common in the term before the child transfers to the reception class of a primary school. Nursery education has value in terms of present benefits to many young children as well as in terms of their preparation for the years of compulsory schooling; in this respect it may particularly help children from disadvantaged backgrounds or with special educational needs. Local education authorities and schools should continue to ensure that children in those two categories of need receive an appropriate share of the available places, at the same time ensuring a balance within individual classes between these and other children. Settling-in procedures may include home visiting, visits to the school and information packs which reinforce the benefits that early schooling brings.

(a) Premises

The extent of teaching and playroom accommodation, other indoor facilities including sanitary accommodation and the area to be provided outside for play, are all covered by the Education (School Premises) Regulations 1981. DES

Design Notes 1 and 11 give advice on the planning of nursery provision. Advice on the adaptation of existing buildings is covered by Building Bulletin 56 and Broadsheet 1.

(b) Staffing

To allow both for the teaching and the administrative workload of headteachers of nursery schools, the minimum staff/child ratios recommended for these institutions is 2:20, one being a qualified teacher and the other a qualified nursery assistant. The corresponding figures for nursery classes are 2:26.

Primary Schools admitting 4-year olds to Reception Classes

6.44. The admission of 4-year olds to reception classes of primary schools is another way to extend the educational opportunities available to these children and make use of the available facilities. Most of these children attend full time though numbers of local education authorities and schools arrange for beginners to do so part time. Studies by HM Inspectorate have shown that the provision made for those who are younger than 4 years 9 months has not always fitted their needs. Among essential requirements for success with these young children are: careful planning of this provision as part of the overall programme of the school; a curriculum serving the immediate requirements of young children and preparing them for further stages in their education; appropriate staff training; and class sizes that are manageable taking account of the age range of the children and the number of adults available to teach them. Local education authorities and schools should determine what staffing levels may be appropriate in particular cases. Quality however should not be put at risk in pursuing further development in the quantity of provision.

Combined Centres

6.45. Combined centres provide day care and nursery education in the same unit. They are usually run by social services and education departments as a joint responsibility but vary in their approaches. Organisational forms also vary depending chiefly on whether the teacher in charge of the nursery class answers solely to the management of the unit or to the head teacher of a primary school with which the unit is linked.

(a) Premises

The same principles apply as for day nurseries etc.

(b) Staffing

Local authorities should decide what management structure is appropriate in each case. A particular model is not suggested but lines of responsibility should be clear. Among the staff there should be a balance of skills and qualifications in teaching children in the early years, in nursery nursing and in child care; at least 50% of the staff should be qualified. The adult to child ratio will depend on whether the centre caters only for over 3s or for under 3s as well, and whether or not an extended day is provided for children attending for nursery education. Subject to these points local authorities should follow the recommendations for staffing nursery schools and classes so far as the educational provision is concerned. For the remaining provision the recommendations for staffing full and sessional day care should apply as appropriate.

Private Nursery Schools

6.46. A variety of institutions may describe themselves by this title. They have in common that they deal exclusively or almost exclusively with children under 5, and are neither maintained by a local education authority nor administered as an integral part of an independent school, but they differ in the extent and form of their educational provision. For the purpose of registration with social services departments an institution comes within the description of a private nursery school – and is thus distinguished from the generality of day nurseries –

if its distinctive educational emphasis is such as to fulfill each of these conditions:

- it is open for the period of the school day during school term;

- it provides for children in the 3 to 5 age range;

- the children are under the oversight of a qualified teacher (that is, a person who has satisfied the requirements of the Secretary of State for Education and Science for qualified teacher status);

- support is provided by a qualified nursery assistant (that is, a person with the certificate of the National Nursery Examination Board or a comparable qualification).

If the head combines teaching and administrative tasks and, like her peer in maintained nursery schools, is included within the staffing ratios, the minimum staff/child ratio is 2:20. If the head is not engaged in teaching and is excluded from the ratios, the minimum staff/child ratio is 2:26. In either case one must be a qualified teacher and the other a qualified nursery assistant. They must be in post, not simply on the complement. Otherwise a ratio of 1:8 should apply. In all other respects the advice in paragraph 6.41 will be applicable to these institutions. Hence, in respect of lunch hour provision and any after school care the ratios should accord with those for day nurseries.

SECTION D: CHILDMINDING

6.47. Childminders may look after pre-school and school age children. This section also applies to nannies employed to look after the children of more than two sets of parents because they are not exempt from the requirement to register with the local authority. Childminders work in their own homes, usually on their own although some may work with an assistant and some in partnership with another childminder. Some may also provide training opportunities for people on a childcare course – for example an NNEB student – or anyone gaining work experience to work with young children in a domestic setting.

(a) Childminder/child ratio

The standard recommended ratios are:

1:3 children aged under 5

1:6 children aged between 5 and 7

1:6 children aged under 8 of whom no more than 3 are under five.

Where a childminder employs an assistant same ratios apply for the additional children. These ratios apply to nannies employed by more than two sets of parents to look after their children. In all cases the ratios include the childminder's own children. When deciding on the ratios to set local authorities should have regard to the number of children aged over 8 and under 14 who are likely to be in the house regularly. The Act gives local authorities power to set a limit on the number of children within the under 8 age banding and they may wish to use this to apply an upper limit to the number of babies who may be looked after by a childminder.

(b) Premises

The premises should be free from hazards and welcoming to children. There should be sufficient space for children to have undisturbed naps during the day. This might involve using a separate room such as a bedroom which will often not be on the same floor as the living room or kitchen. Where the childminder is working in a house rather than a flat, the access to the garden should be safe and the garden free from hazards. There should be adequate arrangements for the control of pets so that children are not at risk of injury. Where a childminder does not have a garden, she should make arrangements to take the children to local playgrounds or parks regularly.

(c) **Equipment and toys**

Fires, switches, plugs and cookers should be adequately protected so that there is no risk of the children injuring themselves. There should be arrangements for safe storage of items such as ornaments, sharp knives and kitchen equipment which could injure the children or cause an accident. There should be a stairgate and the door to the garden should be secured so that children cannot get out unsupervised or without the knowledge of the childminder. Any door fitted with glass should have safety glass or be covered with protective plastic film. There should be sufficient equipment such as high chairs, bedding and buggies or car seats so that the childminder can provide good quality care. An equipment loan scheme which might be run by the social services department of the local authority or local childminding group is an effective way of ensuring that childminders have access to the amount and type of equipment they need. Childminders should consider how best to ensure that the children they care for can choose from a variety of toys. They will need to ensure also that their own children's toys are kept secure and any toys brought by minded children are returned promptly. Toy libraries provide access to a range of toys which the children can choose for themselves and enable childminders to offer variety to the children.

(d) **Relationship with Parents**

Childminders and parents need to have a clear understanding about the terms and conditions of the arrangement with which both agree. The Departments recommend a written contract to cover such matters as the level of fees, the times for leaving and collecting the child, the arrangements covering sickness in the child, parent and childminder, holidays, child's attendance, where appropriate, at playgroup, pre school education facility or special activity such as swimming, special dietary requirements and policy on behaviour and sanctions. The model contract prepared by the National Childminding Association is commended.

(e) **Observation, Assessment, Records and Reports**

The Act requires childminders to keep records of the children they look after. Local authorities should take account of the advice in paragraph 6.41 about keeping records of observation and assessment of children's activities. As childminders usually work alone in domestic premises maintenance of formal records is not practicable. However they should be able to share with the parents details about what the child has done during the day including any changes in behaviour. This might involve keeping notes as well as relying on memory. Local authorities should encourage childminders to develop these skills.

SECTION E: STANDARDS FOR DAY CARE SERVICES FOR SCHOOL AGE CHILDREN

6.48. Day care services provide play opportunities for school age children outside school hours and in the holidays in three types of setting, which may overlap; a care setting where children are looked after by other adults when the parent is not available; an open access or drop-in play setting where children go to meet other children and where there is some adult supervision; a special interests setting where children develop particular skills and knowledge.

6.49. The Act requires local authorities to regulate day care and supervised activities used by school age children aged under 8 – ie aged between 5 and 7. The section 18 general duty to provide day care which includes supervised activities for children in need and the power to provide such a service for other children, apply to children of any age. These paragraphs deal in detail with the standards which are acceptable for registration purposes for services used by school age children aged under 8. They should also be applied where a service is run on premises which are exempt from the registration requirement or by the social services department of a local authority itself. The services covered are:

- sessional and full day care (out-of-school club and holiday scheme);

- open access facility.
  (see Annex C for descriptions of the different types of service)

6.50. Sessional care facilities normally run after the end of the school day for two or three hours and perhaps for an hour before school. Full day care facilities operate during the holidays and sometimes at half term. Children will be escorted to the facility and will stay there until collected by a parent or someone who has parental responsibility or is looking after the child.

(a) Staff/Child Ratio

The standard recommended ratio is:

1:8 for children aged between 5 and 7.

A higher ratio may be necessary when children with disabilities attend a facility; a lower ratio may be appropriate for some short sessional facilities not lasting the full day. Providers running such facilities should ensure that at least half the staff hold a relevant qualification, for example in child care, teaching, playwork or youth work, and the person in charge must be qualified, unless he has considerable experience. Where facilities are used by children aged over 8 as well as under 8, providers should ensure that there are sufficient staff in total to maintain the 1:8 ratio for the under 8s. In the case of full day care holiday schemes the person in charge should be treated as supernumerary in the calculation of the ratio where there are places for more than 24 children. This does not apply to sessional facilities.

(b) Premises and Space Standards

Facilities may be organised in a variety of places ranging from those designed with the needs of children in mind where the provider is the sole occupant, through shared facilities which are designed for children to non-purpose built accommodation shared with other users. The space standard for children aged under 8 should be 25 square feet of clear space per child (2.3 square metres). Regard should be had to the number of older children likely to be present, and whether children with disabilities attend. There should be some office space, facilities for providing snacks or main meals (according to the type of facility and its operational policy), toilet facilities (a minimum of 1 lavatory and wash basin per 10 children and separate facilities for staff). Where possible, providers should be able to separate boisterous and quiet activities. This is particularly important for facilities used by the same children all day. There should also be access to outside playspace preferably adjacent to the premises. Where this is not possible, local parks and other open spaces should be used.

(c) Number of Places and Group Size

There is insufficient information available to advise on maximum numbers. Organisers need to give careful consideration to this point and in so doing consider such points as viability, and likely catchment area. In care settings where children are likely to remain for two hours and more during the holidays, high overall numbers may mean that proportionately fewer children receive individual attention regardless of the actual staff/child ratios. It is suggested that where a very large facility is concerned – with over 100 places for example – it should be organised so that the children are in self-contained units of not more than 30. The group size of children aged under 8 should not normally exceed ten.

(d) Visits and Outings

These are likely to add to the children's interest and enjoyment. This applies particularly to holiday schemes, but out of school clubs may also wish to arrange occasional visits to local facilities such as swimming baths, skating rink or library. The arrangements for transporting the children need to be carefully planned and, where necessary, additional people recruited to ensure safety. This is particularly important where children with disabilities are concerned. There must be agreed arrangements for obtaining parental permission in writing for outings and visits. The use of consent forms is commended.

(e) Furniture and Equipment

This should be suitable, in reasonable repair and well maintained. Providers may wish to supplement chairs with beanbags and floor cushions which help create a friendly and informal atmosphere. Equipment and materials should be in sufficient supply for the number of children attending or likely to attend. It should include materials for art, collage, sport and games, dressing up, music, jigsaws, construction toys and crafts.

(f) Observation, Assessment, Reports and Records

The Act requires registered providers to maintain records of the children attending any facility but this will be limited to factual matters. It is desirable for people working with children in out-of-school or holiday settings to develop skills in observing what the children are doing and to assess the implications in terms of child development and planning future activities. Providers should decide whether to adopt a policy of having written records in order to help development of this skill.

Open Access Facilities

6.51. There is a variety of such facilities. The important distinguishing feature of all of them is that there is no limit on the numbers of children who may attend and the providers do not undertake to keep the child until he is collected by a parent or other adult who has parental responsibility or is looking after the children. Open access facilities are a valuable resource because they add to the variety of services available and their more informal nature may offer children as they grow older more scope to develop confidence and social skills. Children aged between 5 and 7 may enjoy such informal play opportunities but open access facilities need to be organised so as to prevent this younger age group coming to harm and to ensure that they are well cared for.

(a) Staff/Child Ratio

Providers should use the ratio of 1:8 as a guideline in order to ensure that the 5 to 7 year olds are not overwhelmed by the older children. That might mean ensuring adequate numbers of staff to organise activities targeted on the younger children.

(b) Premises and Space Standards

Open access facilities may be provided in local parks or playgrounds as well as in places such as community centres, village halls or leisure centres. It is inappropriate to lay down precise space standards. The guideline of 25 square feet (2.3 square metres) per child aged 5 to 7 in 6.50(b) above should be taken into account by providers and local authorities when deciding on the operational policy and the requirements to be imposed on a registered person.

(c) Number of Places and Group Size

Providers need to ensure that the overall numbers likely to attend a facility at any one time do not put children at risk of injury or accident. The 5-7 year olds are more vulnerable than the older children particularly when the facility becomes crowded. When preparing the programme of activities attention should be given to enabling small groups of children to work together.

(d) Furniture and Equipment

The advice in 6.50(e) is applicable to open access facilities.

(e) Observation, Assessment, Reports and Records

The Act requires registered persons to maintain records of the children attending a facility and the people employed. Providers should also ensure that staff develop some observational and assessment skills so that they can identify activities which are successful and aspects needing improvement or modification.

CHAPTER 7 — REGISTRATION OF DAY CARE SERVICES AND CHILDMINDING

7.1. Chapter 5 gives advice on the local authority's role. This Chapter gives advice on implementation of Part X of and Schedule 9 to the Act.

7.2. Local authorities are responsible for deciding in the first instance whether or not an applicant should be registered under the Act. Each application should be dealt with on an individual basis and the legislation applied according to the particular circumstances of the case.

7.3. The duty to carry out the registration function rests with the local authority which, under the provisions of the Local Authority Social Services Act 1970 and Schedule 13 paragraph 26 to the Children Act, is required to refer the matter to the Social Services Committee. The function cannot be referred to another committee and cannot be exercised by an outside organisation on a contractual or agency basis. While the duty to exercise the registration function lies with the social services department of the local authority, the policy on registration should be approved by the local authority as a whole. In developing the policy, social services departments together with other relevant departments in local authorities should see this as an enabling process which helps intending providers and childminders offer good quality services to parents and children with the minimum of bureaucracy but with adequate support and encouragement.

7.4. Requirements imposed under section 72 (Childminders) and section 73 (Day Care) should be limited to those set out in the Act as mandatory and such others as are essential for the proper provision of the service. Local authorities will also wish to advise on and look for standards of good practice, but it is important to maintain a clear distinction between what is obligatory for registration purposes and suggestions for improving the service.

THE REGISTRATION SYSTEM

7.5. The Act gives local authorities a duty to maintain a register of day care providers and childminders. It is for local authorities to decide how to set up and operate the registration system. This should involve all relevant departments within the local authority, and in the case of shire counties with the district councils within their area as well. Senior officers will wish to be involved in setting up and monitoring the system.

7.6. In devising the registration system local authorities should have regard to the need for:

- a systematic approach to the task so that applications are dealt with quickly and efficiently;

- staff responsible for processing applications and assessing standards of care to have appropriate training and adequate support;

- intending and actual applicants to be given comprehensive information about the process, including the time it will take and what is expected of them.

The Legal Department

7.7 It is essential to involve the Legal Department closely in setting up the registration system so that there are agreed procedures for seeking legal advice. These should identify the circumstances when the Legal Department must be consulted before a particular step is taken and when this might be advisable. The publication **Registration of Childminding and Day Care: Using the Law to raise Standards** (HMSO forthcoming) is commended to the attention of local authorities.

The Education Department

7.8. Section 27 of the Act gives local authorities power to seek help from other authorities including local education authorities in relation to their responsibilities towards children in need. Paragraph 8 of Schedule 9 to the Act gives the social services departments of local authorities power to ask for assistance from local education authorities if it seems to them that this would help the exercise of any of the functions covered in Part X. Where such a request is made, local education authorities are under a duty to supply the help, provided it is compatible with their statutory and other duties and does not prejudice the carrying out of other functions.

7.9. This new power gives social services departments of the local authority the necessary legal force to look for advice on the educational element when they register private and voluntary day care services and childminders and when they inspect registered persons. This is particularly important in the case of services used by 3 and 4 year olds. Proprietors of private nursery schools are required to be registered with social services departments. In assessing the fitness of the person proposing to run a private nursery school, the registration officer needs to have regard to educational matters and therefore he should seek advice from the education department before granting registration.

7.10. In registering private and voluntary day nurseries where the primary purpose is to care for children for the length of the adult working day, attention also needs to be paid to the educational element so that children attending these facilities are able to develop an appropriate range of skills in preparation for full time education. Before registering childminders, local authorities should satisfy themselves about their understanding of child development, how children learn and what activities can enhance the process. Where necessary they should seek advice from education departments of local authorities. Services used by school age children may have a less specific educational focus but the programme of activities should be broadly complementary to the school curriculum. This may require some understanding of the National Curriculum and the educational aspects of recreational activities.

7.11. Social services and education departments in local authorities need to agree on the policy and mechanism for using this power. In so doing they should have regard to the advice in Chapter 5 on the arrangements for drawing together the different local authority functions in this area and to the guidance in Chapter 9 on the review duty.

Libraries, Recreation and Leisure

7.12. These departments in a Metropolitan Council or London Borough provide services – particularly play opportunities – used by young children, and are a useful source of advice on such matters. There should be agreed arrangements and procedures for seeking their advice. In some parts of the country both shire counties and district councils provide such services for children and there should also be agreed arrangements and procedures for seeking advice where necessary.

Planning Departments

7.13. It is essential that social services departments of local authorities and the planning departments (District Councils in the case of the shire counties) establish working arrangements which enable each to have a clear understanding about the other's policy and operation. There is considerable flexibility within the planning system but it is recommended that intending day care providers contact the planning department or District Council at an early stage to discuss their proposals. The aim should be to ensure that the planning process does not unduly hinder completion of the registration process.

Fire Departments

7.14. Social services and fire departments within the local authority need to establish working arrangements so that each understands the other's policy and procedures. It is recommended that social services departments consult fire departments before granting registration. Fire departments will be prepared to inspect the premises and advise social services departments about fire safety as well as giving advice to the person who has applied for registration.

Environmental Health and Food Safety

7.15. Social services departments within local authorities need to establish effective working arrangements with environmental health departments within the local authority, or in the case of shire counties with the District Councils, so that there is clear understanding about each other's policy and procedures. Environmental Health Officers are a useful source of advice on food hygiene and food safety matters as well as other aspects relating to environmental health. Social services departments should also ensure that environmental health officers clearly understand that childminding is a service provided in domestic premises.

Health and Safety

7.16. Social services departments should establish effective working relationships with the local office or offices of the Health and Safety Inspectorate.

7.17. Annex D contains brief notes on planning matters, fire regulations, food safety and health and safety issues.

Police Departments

7.18. Circular LAC(88)19 issued jointly with Home Office, Department of Education and Science and Welsh Office gives advice about the arrangements for checking with local police forces the possible criminal background of those who apply to work with children. The list in the circular aims to identify the main groups and is not intended to be exhaustive. Childminders and other adults in the household are included in the list as one of the main groups to whom the arrangements apply. Social services departments in local authorities should ensure that they establish close working relationships with police departments so that the arrangements for carrying out the police checks do not unduly delay completion of the registration process.

Handling of Applications

7.19. Local authorities should ensure that decisions on applications for registrations are normally reached within **3 months** of receipt of the completed application form in the case of childminders and providers of sessional day care (playgroups, out of school clubs) and **six months** in the case of full day care services. Where there is likely to be a delay the applicant should be informed of the reasons and told when the decision is likely to be made.

Staffing

7.20. The Act introduces a common age limit of under 8 which is to apply to people providing day care for children in non-domestic premises and childminders working in domestic premises. This change may require people who have been responsible for registering services used by under fives to acquire knowledge about services used by older children. Local authorities should consider the implications of the new age limit for registration staff in the light of the views of the staff concerned and the resources available.

Workload

7.21. Local authorities should decide on the appropriate workload for registration officers, having regard to their policy on day care and related services for families with young children. The following factors are relevant when working out what staff are needed to run an efficient registration system:

- the recommended time limits for completion of the process set out in paragraph 7.19 above;
- quantity and type of existing facilities in the area;
- the likely rate of new applications and for what type of service;
- average number of visits made to intending day care providers before process is complete;
- average number of visits made to intending childminders before process is complete;
- average amount of administrative work (telephone calls, letters etc) associated with each application;
- some allowance for dealing with more complex applications;
- volume of enquiries from intending providers or childminders;
- support visits to registered persons;
- inspection duty;
- administrative support (eg clerical help, management time).

The registration system should be organised so that the duties of individual staff processing applications are confined to that work. It is also important to ensure adequate management and administrative support. Local authorities should set up arrangements for monitoring the efficiency and effectiveness of the system, including mechanisms for identifying at an early stage increases in numbers of applications, so that remedial action can be taken.

PERSONS REQUIRED TO REGISTER

7.22. The registration system is based on the concept of 'registered persons'. The term 'person' in law covers natural persons and corporate bodies eg companies, organisations such as charities and some committees. Local authorities are not required to keep a separate register of *non-domestic premises* where day care or supervised activities are provided. 'Premises' is defined as including a vehicle. (section 71(1) and (12)).

7.23. There are two categories of person:

(a) a childminder who looks after one or more children aged under 8 *for reward* on domestic premises (section 71(1)(a)(2) and (12)).

(b) A carer who provides day care or supervised activities on non-domestic premises for one or more children aged under 8. Separate registration is necessary for a person who provides a day care service in more than one place. *The for reward criterion does not apply in the case of a person providing day care on non domestic premises* (sections 71(1)(b), (3) and (12)).

7.24. The legislation requires that day care services run by other departments within the local authority and, in shire counties, those run by District Councils are to be registered with the social services department. They should therefore conform to the same requirements and conditions as those organised by independent bodies or individuals. Facilities managed by the social services department of a local authority itself should also conform. In the case of other departments within the local authority the 'registered person' should be the department concerned.

7.25. The term 'day care' covers such facilities as day nurseries, playgroups, permanent creches in shopping centres, leisure centres, further or higher educational establishments, temporary creches set up for special events such as conferences, out of school clubs, holiday playschemes, adventure playgrounds, childminding and nannies (in certain circumstances).

7.26. In Section 18 the term 'day care' includes care or supervised activities provided for children during the day and the same terms are used for out of school provision for school age children. 'Supervised activity' is defined in the Act as one 'supervised by a responsible person'. In the absence of a definition of 'supervise' in the Act local authorities should use the dictionary definition and consult their legal departments when drawing up their policy on registration. The term is not used in Part X which covers day care provided by the private and voluntary sectors who are subject to regulation. Section 18 of the Act is used to cover the provision of activities for children being cared for.

EXEMPTIONS

7.27. The following individuals are exempt:

- a relative (a parent, grandparent, brother, sister, uncle, aunt, a step-parent and by affinity) of the child;
- a person with parental responsibility (within the meaning of section 3);
- a foster parent in respect of the foster child but he is required to register if he looks after other children (section 71(4));
- a person employed by the parent to look after the child mainly in the child's home (section 71(5));
- a person employed by *two* sets of parents to look after the children of both of them in the home of one or other of the children (section 71(7)).

A person employed by more than two sets of parents to look after their children is required to register as a childminder.

7.28. Paragraphs 3 and 4 of Schedule 9 to the Act list the institutions and establishments which are exempt from the requirement to register even though children aged under 8 attend them. These are:

- registered children's homes;
- voluntary children's homes;
- community homes;
- homes registered under the Registered Homes Act 1984;
- NHS hospitals;
- LEA maintained or assisted schools;
- self-governing schools;
- independent schools.

People who provide private nursery schools are required to register with social services departments. Independent schools, a feature of which is that they provide full-time education for five or more pupils of compulsory school age, are required to register with the Department of Education and Science and are subject to inspection by HM Inspectorate of Schools. Persons providing a nursery unit in an independent school which is an integral part of the institution are *not* required to register with social services departments.

7.29. The exempt provision for these institutions does *not* apply where:

- . a person including a voluntary or community group or private company, who is not employed by the organisation managing the institution, is allowed to use part of the building to provide day care;
- the person responsible for the institution or establishment, or someone employed by him, provides a day care service but the service is *not* an integral part of the institution or establishment nor included in the job description of the employee.

This means that where for example an NHS hospital or LEA maintained school allows an outside individual or organisation to run a day care service on its premises, not as part of its activities, it is required to register.

OCCASIONAL DAY CARE FACILITIES

7.30. Paragraph 5 of Schedule 9 provides for day care facilities which are used on less than six days in a year to be exempt from the registration requirement. This exemption is intended to cover day care facilities set up for conferences and other occasional events. In all cases, before using the premises to provide day care for the first time, the organiser has to notify the relevant local authority that a day care facility is being provided. He should give information about its location, the numbers and age range of the children, numbers of staff and opening hours. Local authorities should keep a record of such notifications. It is unnecessary to visit the premises on each occasion but this should be done from time to time so that local authorities may satisfy themselves about the suitability of the premises. Where different organisations use the same premises, the six days apply in respect of each organisation not in respect of the premises.

Time Limit

7.31. Section 71(2) states that registration is required where the day care provider or childminder is offering a service for children aged under 8 for a period or total periods of *more than 2 hours in a day.* This applies irrespective of the time spent in a day care or supervised activity or with a childminder by an individual child. Therefore facilities such as day nurseries and creches in shopping centres, or leisure centres or colleges which are open throughout the day *are registrable,* even though individual children are likely to attend for less than 2 hours.

FIT PERSON

7.32. Section 71(7) and (8) define two categories of fit person. Where the person is proposing to look after children age under 8 the social services department of the local authority has to be satisfied that he is 'fit' – ie suitable – to do this. The local authority has to satisfy itself that other people living or working on the premises are 'fit to be in the proximity of children aged under 8'. The local authority should have regard to these points when considering whether someone is fit to look after children aged under 8:

- previous experience of looking after or working with young children or people with disabilities or the elderly;
- qualification and/or training in a relevant field such as child care, early years education, health visiting, nursing or other caring activities;
- ability to provide warm and consistent care;
- knowledge of and attitude to multi-cultural issues and people of different racial origins;
- commitment and knowledge to treat all children as individuals and with equal concern;
- physical health;
- mental stability, integrity and flexibility;
- known involvement in criminal cases involving abuse to children.

With persons living or working on the premises the points are:
- previous records;
- known involvement in criminal cases involving abuse to children.

Local authorities should use the above list as a basis for deciding on the fitness of an applicant for registration. Persons applying for registration should know what factors are being considered when their fitness is being assessed.

7.33. Section 71(11) requires the local authority to satisfy itself about the fitness – ie suitability – of the premises – domestic and non-domestic – before granting registration. In considering suitability the local authority is to look at situation, construction and size. The type of premises used will vary considerably and each authority should decide for itself whether particular premises satisfy their criteria for suitability having regard to location, type of building and size. The local authority is to have regard to the points in lists (a) and (b) below when deciding on the suitability of premises for caring for children aged under 8. Persons applying for registration should know what factors are being considered when assessing the suitability of premises.

(a) **Domestic Premises**

- access to garden and safety within it (fencing of ponds for example) and access to the road (children should be unable to leave the premises unsupervised);
- outside playspace;
- safety of fires, electrical sockets, windows, floor coverings and glass doors (safety glass or protective plastic film should be used);
- cooking facilities and safety in the kitchen or cooking area;
- use of stairgates;
- presence of pets and arrangements for their control;
- arrangements for keeping the premises clean; facilities for rest and sleep;
- washing and toilet facilities and hygiene;
- fire safety eg smoke detectors, matches locked away.

While there is no statutory requirement to consult the fire department before granting registration to a childminder, this may be advisable. The risks of a child aged under five dying in a fire in domestic premises is over four times that of an adult aged under 60. One in nine fire deaths in the home is of a child under five although surveys indicate that these have been the result of fires occurring during the night. Childminders might be encouraged to do fire safety training. An intending childminder who lives in a flat above ground level must not be refused registration on the grounds that the premises are not 'fit' because they are above street level and/or outside playspace is not adjacent.

(b) **Non-domestic Premises**

The advice in chapter 6 on space standards and organisation of room or rooms in services used by under fives and school age children should be taken into account in addition to these factors:

- access to road (children should be unable to leave the premises unsupervised) and outside playspace;
- safety in the outside play area;
- glass doors (safety glass or protective plastic film should be used);
- arrangements for arrival and departure;
- washing, toilet facilities and hygiene;
- safety of fires, electric sockets, windows, floor coverings;
- cooking facilities and safety in the kitchen area;
- arrangements for keeping the premises clean;
- facilities for rest and sleep.

The local authority should consult the fire department before granting registration. Fire officers will be able to advise day care providers about the use of fire fighting equipment, exit doors fitted with panic bolts and latches and rapid evacuation of children. It is suggested that day care providers should be encouraged to use this source of advice. There is no objection to having a day care facility above the ground floor. If a provider wishes to use more than one floor, there should be proper arrangements for safeguarding access to the stairs or lifts. Registration should never be refused on the grounds that the facility was to be on the first floor or higher.

EQUIPMENT

7.34. Section 71(11) gives a local authority power to refuse registration if it considers that any equipment on the premises in question is not fit having regard to condition, situation, construction and size. There are different sources of advice on the safety of different types of equipment and registration officers should ensure that they are kept informed about these. In their examination of the equipment in a day care facility or a childminder's home local authorities should take account of these points:

* the equipment should be appropriate to the ages and stages of the children;

* where a British Standard exists, the equipment and furniture should conform to it;

* the amount of equipment and furniture and their quality and type should be adequate for the number of children attending the facility and the adults working there;

* the organisation of kitchen equipment in *non-domestic* premises must comply with environmental health regulations.

NON-PARENTAL CARE OF BABIES AND TODDLERS

7.35. Under the provisions of the Act local authorities have a duty to register persons providing day care in non-domestic premises who intend to offer places for babies and toddlers provided that they satisfy the requirements regarding their own fitness and suitability of premises and equipment. In deciding on the requirements to be imposed, with which registered persons must comply, local authorities should pay particular attention to these points in addition to the advice in paragraphs 7.39 to 7.43 below:

* separate room for babies and toddlers;

* organisation of staff rotas so that there is as much continuity of carer as possible;

* each baby to be looked after by one person during each shift;

* knowledge of child development in the very young and understanding about ways of enhancing development of skills through interaction, play etc.

MOBILE FACILITIES (PLAYBUSES)

7.36 There are particular points to be considered in the case of day care services provided on playbuses. These include the organisation and lay out of the space, access to the stairs (in the case of double deckers), hand rails on stairs, access to the driver's cab and exit/entry doors, fire precautions and safety generally. Many mobile facilities are used by a range of client groups and use of the space is planned on that basis.

REGISTRATION REQUIREMENTS

7.37. Sections 72 (childminders) and 73 (day care providers) set out the requirements which local authorities must impose on a person's registration and with which the registered person must comply. Local authorities have discretion to impose other requirements which must not conflict with the mandatory requirements. In deciding on the requirements to be imposed local authorities are to treat each case individually so that the requirements reflect its particular circumstances.

7.38. The mandatory requirements relate to:

- numbers of children;
- maintenance and safety of the premises and equipment;
- maintenance of records;
- notification of changes;
- numbers of staff (day care providers only).

Numbers of Children

7.39. Chapter 6 contains detailed advice on this which should be followed when deciding on the requirements to impose on the registered person. Local authorities should ensure a flexible approach to this matter.

Maintenance and Safety of Premises and Equipment

7.40. Local authorities should take account of guidance in paragraphs 7.33 and 7.34 above and that in Chapter 6 on standards of services when imposing requirements. Day care providers and childminders should be encouraged to pay proper attention to this aspect so that children are cared for safely. Local authorities should satisfy themselves about registered persons' knowledge and understanding of safety issues and use of sources of advice and, where appropriate, access to training.

Records

7.41. Registered persons must keep records of the following:

- names and addresses of children attending or being looked after;
- names and addresses of staff (in the case of day care providers) or assistants (in the case of childminders);
- in the case of childminders names of people living or likely to be living in the house;
- names of the members of the Board of Directors, management committee or group (in the case of day care providers).

The records about the child should include age/date of birth, name by which he is known and birth name (if different) and surname, names of parents, emergency telephone numbers and information about health problems or conditions (if any) and whether he is on any medication. This last point is particularly important in the case of children in full day care or with a childminder, and may be desirable in some instances (eg where children with disabilities are concerned) for children attending sessional day care. In the case of childminders details about other adults in the house should include the immediate family, any lodgers or subtenants, or live-in employees. An assistant employed by a childminder is not required to register under the Act.

Numbers of Staff

7.42. This applies to day care providers only. The advice in Chapter 6 on staff/child ratios should be followed. Attention should also be paid to numbers and types of support staff (for example kitchen and cleaning staff, administrative and clerical staff, caretaker). Local authorities should make enquiries about use of volunteers and whether this is done regularly or occasionally.

Notification of Changes

7.43. Registered persons are required to notify changes in the numbers of staff (day care providers) or in the assistants (childminders) looking after the children and people living in the premises. It is suggested that as a matter of good practice childminders should also inform the local authority about major alterations to the premises and if they cease to work as a childminder. On receipt of information about any changes local authorities should decide on the appropriate action to take, such as instituting checks and/or paying a visit. Day care providers are required to report changes in the type of day care offered: for example a pre-school facility which decides to offer an after school service for school age children – and the opening hours – for example where a playgroup which is open for two mornings a week wishes to offer a third morning or extend the hours offered to cover a greater part of the day. On being notified of changes local authorities will wish to consider the need to visit. If they are satisfied that the person and premises still meet the fitness and suitability criteria, a revised certificate should be issued.

DISCRETIONARY REQUIREMENTS

7.44. Sections 72(5) (childminders) and 73(7) (day care providers) give local authorities power to impose other requirements provided these do not conflict with the mandatory requirements. It is for local authorities to decide on their use of this power. Local authorities will wish to consider the need for a general policy on the use of the power so that the registration system provides the framework for good quality services. It is suggested that this power enables the local authority to encourage day care providers and childminders to operate in a businesslike way – for example by taking out public liability insurance – and to raise standards through training.

VARIATION, ADDITION OR CANCELLATION OF IMPOSED REQUIREMENTS

7.45. Section 72(6) (childminders) and section 73(8) (day care providers) give local authorities power to vary, add to or cancel any imposed requirements. This power is provided so that local authorities can respond appropriately either to changes notified by the registered person or matters raised or identified during the inspection.

REFUSAL OF REGISTRATION

7.46. Section 71(7), (8), (9), (10) and (11) gives local authorities power to refuse registration where they are satisfied that:

- the person who intends to care for the children is not fit to do so;
- someone living or likely to be living or working or likely to be working in the household or premises is not fit to be in the proximity of children aged under 8;
- the premises and/or equipment are not suitable.

Paragraph 2 of Schedule 9 disqualifies certain categories of person from registration unless the local authority gives written consent to removal of the disqualification. Paragraph 1(4) of Schedule 9 states that a local authority must register an applicant if the application is properly made and there are no other grounds for refusal. The registration system is to operate on the basis that the local authority has to be able to demonstrate why they are satisfied that a person is not fit and/or the premises and/or equipment are not suitable. Applicants for registration have to provide the information necessary to enable local authorities to satisfy themselves about these matters. Local authorities should seek legal advice before exercising this power. The basis for refusal should be supported by evidence which will stand up in court.

THE REGISTER

7.47. Section 71 requires local authorities to maintain a register of childminders and people who provide day care services. The main purpose of the register is to provide information about the day care services and childminders in the area to parents and other interested parties such as employers. The form in which the register is kept should be decided by each local authority and in so doing these points should be taken into account:

(a) The register should be compiled so that childminders, sessional day care facilities such as playgroups and out of school clubs, and full day care facilities such as day nurseries can be identified separately. It may also be desirable to identify separately social services department day nurseries, those run by other local authority departments, District Councils and other statutory authorities, nurseries run by companies or individuals as business and those run by voluntary organisations. This might apply also to other types of day care or supervised activity.

(b) Each entry should include the name, address, telephone number and number of places. The register should not be kept on open shelves because of the risk of details about these facilities being used in an improper way.

(c) Enquirers need to be able to find out easily where they may consult the register. Local authorities will wish to decide whether it should be kept in one or more places. Notices about where it is kept should be put up in libraries, clinics, doctors' surgeries, health centres, hospitals, leisure and community centres, local businesses and offices and anywhere else which seems appropriate.

(d) The register may be kept on a computer.

PUBLICITY

7.48. Local authorities will wish to ensure that the introduction of the new registration system is given adequate publicity so that intending childminders and providers of day care know about the need for registration and where to go for information. For example, notices might be put up in area offices, clinics, doctors surgeries, health centres, libraries, post offices, advice bureaux, social security offices, job centres. Local papers, radio stations and television networks might also be used to publicise it. Information for intending childminders and day care providers should make clear the advantages of registration such as access to other local authority services as well as saying that it is an offence not to be registered.

APPLICATIONS FOR REGISTRATION

7.49. Paragraph 1 of Schedule 9 requires people applying for registration to do this in accordance with regulations made by the Secretary of State which include providing details about the people helping to look after the children and those living or likely to be living on the particular premises. The application is to be accompanied by whatever registration fee is prescribed in regulations made by the Secretary of State. The regulations on the application and fees will follow separately. Local authorities should design their own application forms and notes of guidance. The form should require the applicant to supply this information:

- name of person, company, committee or group and, in the case of the last 3, a list of the Board of Directors, officers and members of the committee or group;
- address where it is proposed to look after the children together with address for correspondence if different;
- type of service to be provided (childminding, day nursery, private nursery school, playgroup, out of school club, other supervised activity etc);
- in case of day care to be provided on non domestic premises, proposed numbers and age range of children;
- experiences of providing day care or supervised activities and relevant qualifications;
- references;
- health;
- criminal convictions;

- names of members of staff;
- names of other people living on the premises;
- names of other adults in the household (in the case of childminders).

The notes of guidance should explain how the application will be dealt with including arrangements for checking the criminal background, visiting the applicant, the documentation which should be enclosed such as planning permission, fire certificate etc and amount of the prescribed fee.

FOLLOW UP AFTER GRANTING OF REGISTRATION

7.50. The Act requires local authorities to carry out an inspection of a registered person *at least* once a year. It is also desirable to make occasional visits to provide support and advice to registered persons. In this way it will be possible to identify at an early stage areas of concern and remedial action can be instituted more effectively.

CANCELLATION OF REGISTRATION

7.51. Section 74 gives local authorities power to cancel registration in the following circumstances:

(a) the circumstances would justify refusing to register someone as a childminder or provider of day care (section 74(1)(a) and (2)(a));

(b) the care being given to an individual child is considered by the local authority to be seriously inadequate having regard to his needs including his religious persuasion, racial origin and cultural and linguistic background. (section 74(1)(b) and (2)(b));

(c) the person has contravened or failed to comply with a requirement imposed on their registration (section 74(1)(c)(i) and (2)(c)(i));

(d) failure to pay the annual inspection fee (section 74(1)(c)(ii) and (2)(c)(ii));

(e) the condition of the premises is such that they would be justified in refusing registration (section 74(3)) but not where the time limit set has not expired and their condition is because the repairs, alterations or additions have not been done (section 74(4)).

7.52. In their use of this power local authorities should ensure that the evidence produced to justify cancellation under the grounds set out in 7.51(a), (b) and (c) above is capable of standing up to examination in a court. They should always seek advice about a proposed cancellation from their legal departments. While each case has to be handled in the light of particular circumstances, the following factors should be taken into account:

(a) Circumstances which would justify refusal:

- person no longer fit to look after children aged under 8 by reason of attitude to them, standard of care or health;
- persons living in the household not fit to be in the proximity of children aged under 8 by reason of behaviour towards them or attitude;
- premises or equipment not suitable;

Local authorities should use this power flexibly. In particular it is inappropriate to do this because of short term lapses from agreed or intended ratios.

(b) Seriously inadequate care:

- signs of uncaring neglect such as a child being left in dirty nappy for extended periods, inadequate clothing, cold rooms, inappropriate restraint or child left unattended;
- grossly inappropriate types of activity and play opportunities;
- failure to recognise and respond sensitively to child's religious, racial, cultural and linguistic needs;
- gross lack of emotional and physical warmth.

In assessing whether a registered person is failing to recognise and respond sensitively to a child's religious, racial, cultural and linguistic needs, local authorities might consider whether he is being treated less favourably on racial grounds or he is being ridiculed or his dietary needs are not provided for.

EMERGENCY CANCELLATION

7.53. Section 75 gives local authorities power in cases of emergency to apply to the court: to cancel a person's registration; to vary an imposed requirement; to remove or impose a requirement. Any application to the court for such an order has to be accompanied by a written statement of reasons (section 75(3)) but does not require notice of the application to be given to the registered person. The court is required to satisfy itself that the child who is being or may be looked after by the registered childminder or person providing day care is suffering or likely to suffer significant harm. The court has discretion to make the order (section 75(1)(6)). Cancellation of registration or variation or removal or imposition of a requirement are effective from the date of the order. The local authority is responsible for serving notice of the order on the registered person together with a copy of the written statement of reasons (section 75(4)). Local authorities should always seek legal advice before exercising this power. The evidence submitted must be such as to stand up to examination in a court.

CERTIFICATE OF REGISTRATION

7.54. Paragraph 6 of Schedule 9 requires local authorities to issue each registered person with a certificate which has to specify the person's name and address, the address where the service is provided and the requirements imposed by them under section 72 or 73. Amended certificates may be issued. *The registration system should be organised so that once it has been decided to grant registration a certificate is issued immediately.* If a certificate is lost or destroyed, a copy may be issued on payment of a fee, the level to be prescribed by the Secretary of State. Local authorities should design their own certificates, ensuring that all the information is clearly presented.

PAYMENT OF FEES

7.55. Paragraph 1 of Schedule 9 requires each application for registration to be accompanied by the fee prescribed by the Secretary of State. Under paragraph 7 a prescribed fee is also payable for the annual inspection which has to be paid within 28 days of the inspection being carried out. Failure to pay within that time period will result in registration being cancelled.

APPEALS

7.56. Section 77 requires local authorities which under section 74:

- refuse registration;
- cancel registration;
- refuse consent to a person disqualified from registration (paragraph 2 of Schedule 9);
- impose, remove or vary any registration requirements;
- refuse to grant an application for variation or removal of a requirement

at least 14 days before the proposed action to notify the applicant or registered person of their intention and the reasons for it and give him an opportunity to object. If, after hearing the objections, they still decide to take the action proposed, they have to send a notice in writing. The person then has the right of appeal to a court. It is for local authorities in consultation with the legal department and any others with an interest – for example education, recreation and leisure – to have agreed procedures for dealing with objections from applicants or registered persons. This may involve arranging for the objections to be heard by a panel composed of members and senior officers.

OFFENCES

7.57. Section 78 covers offences:

(a) In the case of the offence of looking after children whilst disqualified from registration, a person found guilty on summary conviction would be liable to a term of imprisonment of not more than six months or a fine or both. For all other offences the penalty would be a fine.

(b) In the case of a childminder, it is an offence to look after children aged under 8 whilst unregistered. Where a local authority believes that someone is doing this, they may serve a notice – an 'enforcement notice' – on the person concerned informing him of the requirement to register and saying that he must not look after children aged under 8 for reward until he is registered. If the person contravenes the terms of the notice, he is guilty of an offence. This means that for childminders the act which could lead to charges being brought is not looking after under eights but doing this in defiance of any notice issued by the local authority. This provision is in the Act to deal with persons who occasionally look after children for reward, usually to help a friend or neighbour in an emergency, but do not intend to do this as a business. It is important to ensure that persons who plan to work as childminders clearly understand that they are required to register.

RE-REGISTRATION

7.58. The Nurseries and Child-Minders Regulation Act 1948 is repealed by the Children Act. Paragraphs 33 and 34 of Schedule 14 to the Act contain transitional provisions so that premises and childminders registered with the local authority under the 1948 Act may retain that registration for a period of up to one year of the coming into force of the Children Act. During that 12 month period local authorities should, where appropriate re-register childminders under section 71(1)(a) and persons in respect of non-domestic premises under section 71(1)(b) of the Children Act.

7.59. Local authorities will wish to take steps to ensure adequate publicity is given in their areas to these transitional provisions and to the need for those people registered under the 1948 Act who wish to continue to work as childminders or day care providers to re-register under the new legislation. It is for each local authority to decide how to publicise this and organise the registration process. In so doing they should ensure that existing facilities are not refused registration under the Children Act on the grounds that their existing staffing levels or space standards fall below those recommended in this guidance,provided their overall standards are satisfactory. In such cases where a local authority considers the standards in an existing facility are below those recommended the childminder or day care provider should be given a specified time to reach them. The exact time limit will depend on the particular circumstances of the case,but normally it should be no more than a year.

CHAPTER 8　INSPECTION

8.1. Section 76 gives local authorities a duty to inspect domestic premises in which registered childminders are working and non- domestic premises where day care for children aged under 8 is being provided *at least* once a year. Under section 76(2) they may also authorise someone to enter any premises in their area if they have reasonable cause to suspect that a child is being looked after by a childminder who is not registered and is not exempt from the requirement to register or by an unregistered person providing day care in non-domestic premises. Any person carrying out this inspection duty is required to carry a document authorising him to undertake the task.

8.2. Schedule 9, paragraph 7 to the Act requires local authorities to notify each registered person in advance that an inspection is to be carried out and that they are required to pay the annual inspection fee as prescribed by the Secretary of State in Regulations. The fee is to be paid within 28 days of the inspection. Reasonable notice should be given. Local authorities may also decide to make visits with no advance warning. This might be necessary where the person who had carried out the inspection was concerned to establish that an acceptable standard of care was being provided consistently.

8.3. The Act gives the person carrying out the inspection power to examine the premises, the children being looked after, the arrangements for their welfare and the records which registered persons are required to keep under the provisions of section 72 or section 73 as appropriate. Where the records are kept on computer, its operation may be checked with help from the registered person if required. It is an offence to obstruct the person carrying out the inspection.

EXAMINATION OF PREMISES

8.4. This should involve looking at safety measures such as fireguards, stairgates, access to outside playspace etc, electrical sockets, windows, storage and cooking facilities; hygiene and cleanliness; use of the space or rooms, toilet facilities. Regard should be had to the advice in Chapters 6 and 7 and the officer should satisfy himself that the registered person is properly complying with the requirements imposed in respect of safety.

THE CHILDREN AND THE ARRANGEMENTS FOR THEIR WELFARE

8.5. The officer carrying out the inspection should satisfy himself that the children are being well looked after and the standard of care provided is acceptable having regard to their needs, including their religious persuasion, racial origin and cultural and linguistic background. He should also take account of the general advice in Chapter 6 and where appropriate any voluntary codes of practice.

RECORDS

8.6. The examination of the records should involve checking that these conform to the imposed requirements. It is also desirable that in the course of the inspection the officer makes enquiries to find out about the registered person's policy on observation, assessment, records and reports on the children and how this is implemented.

PURPOSE

8.7. The main purposes of the inspection are:

- to enable the local authority to satisfy itself that services are being provided to an acceptable standard and children are appropriately cared for;

- to provide reassurance to parents about the involvement of the local authority;

- to ensure that the facilities provided are consistent with the information held on the register;

- to encourage day care providers and childminders to raise standards.

Local authorities should develop policy and procedures for exercising their inspection duty in the light of the above. In so doing they should have regard to the power in paragraph 8 of Schedule 9 to seek advice from the local education authority and ensure that there are agreed procedures for doing this where appropriate.

8.8. There should be arrangements for monitoring the effectiveness of inspection. This should be seen as an integral part of the registration process and it should be used to ensure high standards of service. Registration is granted after visits and discussion with the person concerned but before the day care service opens or the childminder looks after any children. Inspection provides an opportunity for local authorities to satisfy themselves about the quality of services offered by observing the interaction between the adult or adults and the children, and other relevant matters.

PROCESS

8.9. Carrying out an inspection requires particular skills. It is important that staff are given appropriate opportunities to develop knowledge and understanding of the process. This may involve training through seminars and workshops.

8.10. Each inspection should cover the same aspects. It is suggested that a written checklist provides an effective way of ensuring consistency between members of staff and across different facilities. There should be a written report of each inspection visit which should include details about how the room or rooms were organised, what the children were doing and the range of activities offered, the staff or childminder's interaction with the child or children, the arrangements for meals and rests and Health and Safety aspects. The guidance on the review duty says that information derived from the exercise of the inspection duty will enable social services and education departments of the local authority to draw initial conclusions about use of services. The procedures set up for the discharge of the inspection duty should enable local authorities to formulate a general picture about the level and type of services within their areas. There should be agreed arrangements for exchange of information between staff responsible for the inspection and for carrying out the review.

8.11. Local authorities should ensure that the workload carried by people responsible for regulating services used by under 8s takes account of this inspection duty. Apart from the time taken to visit the facility or childminder, there should be adequate administrative support for issuing notifications in good time and report writing. Effective exercise of the inspection duty (together with the registration duty) requires staff to be knowledgeable about the care of young children and the optimum environment for development of skills as well as the techniques of registration and inspection. It is for local authorities to decide how best to achieve this. The independent Inspection Units being set up under the NHS and Community Care Act 1990 are likely to develop considerable knowledge about the technique of registration and inspection. Where appropriate arrangements should be made to enable staff responsible for registering and inspecting providers of day care services and childminders to benefit from this specialised knowledge.

CHAPTER 9   THE REVIEW DUTY

9.1. The review duty in section 19 gives legislative support to Government policy that the level, pattern and range of day care and related services for young children should be worked out at local level by local authorities in consultation with health authorities, voluntary organisations, employer interests, parents and other interested bodies and individuals. Local authorities and local education authorities (in this chapter the phrase' two authorities' is used to cover these) should, jointly, decide how to discharge this duty and, in so doing, they should have regard to these points which also apply to the arrangements for co-ordination generally:

- members should be involved in the process;

- senior officers in the two authorities should consider whether any additional structures or working arrangements are needed to facilitate a co-ordinated approach;

- effective working relationships should be created and maintained with other departments in the authority such as planning, housing, leisure, recreation and libraries, (in the case of shire counties this will require working with District Councils). It is particularly important where services for older children are concerned for the two authorities to work closely with leisure and recreation departments because the latter have considerable knowledge and experience of the services used;

- effective working relationships should be established and maintained with relevant health authorities, other statutory bodies such as District Councils in shire county areas, voluntary organisations, the private sector, employers and parents.

9.2. Section 19 of the Act requires the two authorities to undertake the review as a joint exercise. In the process they are to review all the day care services in the area – those they run themselves, those in the independent sector and childminding – to take account of the nursery and primary education facilities and day care services provided in institutions exempt from the requirement to register and to consult the local health authority and others during the process. A report of the review is to be published and to include information about changes in services and related matters.

9.3. The review should cover day care services and supervised activities for 5-7 year olds. At present such services are not well developed, but it is likely that this will change as more parents return to paid employment as their children grow older. The review process enables any expansion of services for this age group to be properly co-ordinated.

9.4. Section 19(2) requires the review to be conducted at least once every three years. The first review has to be carried out *within a year* of the commencement of the Act.

9.5. There should be arrangements for exchange of information between those involved in the work on the review duty and discharge of the local authorities' general duty to provide day care for children in need, so that the review pays attention to the services which might be used by children in need and local authorities' responsibilities towards such children in need and their families are taken into account.

9.6. The legislation does not require the two authorities to review nursery or primary education facilities as such but they are required to inform themselves about the quantity and availability. This also applies to facilities provided in establishments such as children's homes, NHS hospitals or on Crown premises which are exempt from the requirement to register.

9.7. Section 19(7) requires the two authorities to 'have regard to representations from health authorities and any other representations which they consider relevant'. The two authorities should agree on the arrangements for seeking views from all interested parties and individuals including health authorities at the appropriate levels and sectors. The review should be an open process and early involvement is recommended with health authorities, voluntary bodies such as local PPA groups, childminding interests, community groups, lone parent organisations and ethnic minority groups, with the private day care sector, employers and parents. The model of an under fives forum with members drawn from a wide range of organisations, which some local authorities have developed, is an effective way of consulting and involving outside interests. This model which could be expanded to cover services used by under eights is recommended.

9.8. The purpose of the consultation exercise is to enable the organisations and individuals who are interested in services for young children and their families to give the two authorities their views on the existing pattern of services, the need for changes (if any) and/or developments and how these might be instituted. The two authorities will not wish to limit the matters on which those consulted are asked to comment or express views, but the exercise is likely to be more productive where they suggest the points or services which are causing them concern as well as those aspects which they consider work well.

9.9. In implementing section 19(6)(c) (the proposals for changes to services and related matters) the two authorities should cover the day care services managed by the social services department and, as far as possible, independent services in the area. The review should also cover local authority policy on implementing section 18(3) of the Act – power to provide facilities such as advice, training, guidance and counselling to day care providers, childminders and parents. Where possible a date or time limit should be attached to any changes or developments reported.

THE REVIEW PROCESS

9.10. The concept of 'review' involves measurement or assessment. This is not possible without agreed aims and objectives for the service or services in question so that the review is undertaken within a framework. The process of review should be preceded by establishment of the appropriate structures and the setting of policy aims and objectives. It should be recognised that it is not a one-off exercise.

9.11. The two authorities are responsible for devising their own procedures for carrying out the review, bearing in mind that these should be the main stages in the process:

- setting the terms of reference;
- assembling basic data;
- analysis;
- consultation;
- preparing the report;
- publication and dissemination of the report;
- follow up.

Setting the terms of reference

9.12. The two authorities should agree on detailed terms of reference for the review. This part of the process should include agreeing how the detailed work is to be done and the arrangements for overseeing it. It is suggested that senior officers and members will wish to oversee and steer the work.

Basic Data

9.13. The two authorities, by virtue of their statutory duties and powers, will be able to assemble factual information about numbers of places in day care services (full day care and sessional care for pre-school and school age children) and with childminders, numbers of children attending maintained nursery schools and classes and reception classes in primary schools. These data will include numbers of facilities and the places in them, the different types of provider, (eg social services, other local authority departments, voluntary groups, community or self-help groups, employers, partnerships). The exercise of the registration function will enable social services departments of local authorities to draw conclusions about rates of new applications, time taken to process them and, possibly, mismatches between supply and demand for services in particular places. The exercise of the inspection duty will enable social services departments to draw some initial conclusions about use of services and experiences offered to the children. Social services departments of local authorities should ensure that information about the extent to which they have used the section 18(3) power to provide facilities such as training, advice, guidance and counselling to parents and carers and how, is assembled as part of the data collection. The local authority statistical service will be able to supply data on population, and other demographic information including birth rates, numbers of local authority staff and economic activity and the urban/rural make-up of the area.

Analysis

9.14. The basic data outlined above will enable the two authorities to produce a picture of existing services and the socio-economic context. This should be used as a starting point for analysing how this compares with known policy objectives on day care and early years education and points of concern. Innovative or unusual schemes should be clearly identified as well as centres of excellence and known mismatches between supply and demand and other problems such as recruitment. The analysis should involve examination of issues such as type of curriculum or programme, variations in group size, physical environment including health and safety, staff development and training, multi-cultural and equal opportunities aspects, parental involvement and the policy on day care for children in need and how this is implemented and monitored. Attention should be paid to other support services for parents (eg toy libraries, befriending or home visiting schemes, parent/toddler groups, information services).

Consultation

9.15. The two authorities should work out their consultation procedures in the light of local circumstances. They should give organisations and individuals a reasonable amount of time to respond, but it is suggested that this should never exceed *three months*. Attention should be paid to ways of seeking views from a cross-section of the population. It is suggested that, where there are local umbrella groups or an Under Fives Forum, they should be invited to nominate someone to respond on their behalf. This also applies to organisations representing different ethnic minority groups in the area.

Preparation of the Report

9.16. The two authorities should aim to produce a succinct report which is accessible to a wide audience. This may involve producing it in other languages besides English.

Publication and Dissemination

9.17. The two authorities should decide for themselves the form of publication and the arrangements for dissemination. In so doing they should have regard to these general points:

- the report should help to increase interest in services for young children among the population as a whole;

- it should encourage debate about local services and how their developments can produce benefits;

- the review process should be a continuing one.

Section 19(6) requires the two authorities to publish the results of the review as soon as is reasonably practicable. The two authorities should publish the report no later than three months after the closing date for the consultation exercise. It should be made readily available by, for example, putting notices about it in libraries, area offices, clinics, doctors' surgeries, health centres, hospitals, schools, community centres and church and village halls. The two authorities should ensure that all the organisations and individuals who contributed to the review receive copies.

Follow up

9.18. There should be agreed arrangements for follow-up. These will depend on a number of factors including the type of co-ordination machinery and arrangements within the relevant departments for monitoring policy development. The review process needs to be seen as an active procedure which encourages development of good quality services planned and delivered in the light of local wishes and expectations. Agreed, well publicised arrangements for follow-up will help this to happen.

CONTENT OF THE REPORT

9.19. There should be some consistency as between local authorities in carrying out their duties under the Act. To this end each local authority should ensure that the report of the review covers these matters:

- basic data on services in the area;

- map of the area with the location of facilities marked;

- policies on day care and early years education, children in need, services for children with special educational needs, policies on equal opportunities including race, gender, disability and how developed and monitored;

- centres of excellence and those with innovative or unusual features;

- known problems – for example, mismatch of supply and demand, difficulties in staff recruitment, shortage of childminders or difficulties in the operation of the registration system;

- training opportunities;

- range of other support services for families (toy libraries, home visiting schemes, parent/toddler groups, information services);

- method of conducting the review with details about whether members and senior officers were involved and in what way and the consultation procedures used;

- numbers of local authority staff involved in services for under fives and out of school and in what capacity;

- changes in provision and plans for the future and monitoring arrangements.

FAMILY SUPPORT

Fisher, M., Marsh. P, Phillips, D and Sainsbury, E., **In and Out of Care,** Batsford, 1986

Gardner, R., **Preventing Family Breakdown,** National Childrens Bureau, 1988

Gibbons, J., **Purposes and Organisation of Preventive Work with Families: The Two Area Study** NISW 1989

De-Ath, E., **Self Help and Family Centres,** National Childrens Bureau, 1985

Heywood, J., and Allen B., **Financial Help in Social Work** Manchester University Press, 1971

Jackson, M., P., and Valenca, E., **Financial Aid through Social Work,** Routledge Kegan and Paul 1979

Holman, R., **Putting Families First,** MacMillan, 1988

Packman, J., **The Childs Generation,** Blackwell, 1981

Packman, J., **Who Needs Care,** Blackwell, 1986

Phelan, J., **Family Centres,** The Children's Society 1983

Mellucio, A., **Permanency Planning for Children** Tavistock, 1986£

Hardicker, P., **Purposes and Organisation of Preventive Work with Families,** University of Leicester, 1990

DAY CARE

Moss P., **Review of Childminding Research,** Thomas Coram Research Unit, occasional paper: No 5 Institute of Education, University of London, 1987

Moss P. and Melhuish T, **Current Issues in Day Care for Young Children,** papers from a Conference at London University 27-28 Feb 1990, HMSO, 1991

Schaffer R H **Making Decisions about Children, Psychological Questions and Answers,** Basil Blackwell, Oxford, 1990

Bone M, **Pre-school Children and the Need for Day Care,** OPCS Social Survey, London, HMSO, 1977

Elfer P., Beasley G., **Registration of Childminding and Day Care: Using the Law to raise Standards** HMSO forthcoming

EDUCATION

Clark Margaret M, **Children Under Five, Educational Research and Evidence,** Gordon and Breach Science Publishers, 1988

Department of Education and Science, **Starting With Quality, Report of the Committee of Inquiry into the Quality of the Educational Experience offered to 3 and 4 year olds,** chaired by Mrs Angela Rumbold CBE MP, HMSO, London 1990

H M Inspectorate of Schools, **The Education of Children Under Five** HMSO, 1989

Tizard M and Hughes M, **Young Children Learning: Talking and Thinking at Home and School,** Fontana, London, 1984

H M Inspectorate of Schools, **A Survey of the Quality of Education of Four Year Olds in Primary Classes,** DES, 1989

H M Inspectorate of Schools, **Combined Provision for the Under Fives: The Contribution of Education,** DES, 1988

What Children Learn in Playgroup – A PPA Guide to the Curriculum. Pre-School Playgroups Association 1991

Guidelines for Good Practice for Young Children in Group Day Care. National Children's Bureau (forthcoming).

Guidelines: Good Practice for Full Daycare Playgroups. Pre-School Playgroups Association 1989

Guidelines: Good Practice for Sessional Playgroups. Pre-School Playgroups Association 1989

Guidelines of Good Practice for Out of School Care Schemes. National Out of School Alliance* 1989

*Now the Kids Clubs Network.

Setting the Standards: Guidelines of Good Practice in Registering Childminders. National Childminding Association (forthcoming).

PARENTAL RESPONSIBILITY

1.1. The law gives a collection of rights, powers. duties and responsibilities to parents. In the Act these are referred to collectively as 'parental responsibility'. Under the old law, the rules which governed who may acquire parental responsibility and when it could be exercised were unclear, particularly if a child was subject to a custody order. Only in certain matters, such as the right to withhold agreement to a child's adoption or the right to inherit property when a child dies, has the law been specific.

1.2. The courts have come to regard parental responsibility as a collection of powers and duties which follow from being a parent and bringing up a child. rather than as rights which may be enforced at law. The exercise of parental responsibility is left largely to the discretion of the adults involved, subject to two limitations. First, the criminal law imposes minimum standards of care and civil law provides remedies for the protection of children's welfare [Children and Young Persons Acts 1933 and 1969 and Children Act 1989]. Secondly, parental responsibility itself diminishes as the child acquires sufficient understanding to make his own decisions [Gillick v. West Norfolk and Wisbech Area Health Authority [1986] A.C. 112]. It would not be realistic or desirable to attempt to prescribe in statute the content of parental responsibility. However, the Act does put on a consistent basis rules about who acquires parental responsibility, when it may be exercised and what effect an order under the Act will have upon this.

1.3. 'Parental responsibility' is defined to include all the rights, powers, authority and duties of parents in relation to a child and his property [section 3(1)]. The value of the term parental responsibility is twofold. First, it unifies the many references in legislation to parental rights, powers and the rest. Secondly, it more accurately reflects that the true nature of most parental rights is of limited powers to carry out parental duties.

1.4. The effect of having parental responsibility is to empower a person to take most decisions in the child's life (subject to the limitations mentioned above). It does not make him a parent or relative of the child in law, for example to give him rights of inheritance, or to place him under a statutory duty to maintain a child [section 3(4)].

Who has Parental Responsibility?

1.5. Where a child's parents were or have been married to each other at or after the time of his conception, they each have parental responsibility for him [section 2(1), as extended by section 1 of the Family Law Reform Act 1987, section 2(3)]. Otherwise, the mother alone has parental responsibility unless the father acquires it by a court order or an agreement under the Act [section 2(2)].

1.6. The father who does not have parental responsibility may acquire it in one of two ways:

(a) with the mother, he may make 'a parental responsibility agreement'; or

(b) he may apply to court for an order which gives him parental responsibility [section 4(1)].

1.7. A parental responsibility agreement was not available under the old law (although a parent could make an agreement about the exercise of her parental rights and duties under section 1(2) of the Guardianship Act 1973). It is intended as a simple and cheap method by which unmarried parents may share parental responsibility without going to court. The agreement must be made in the form prescribed by regulations and, if further regulations are made. will have to be officially recorded in the prescribed manner [section 4(2)]. The effect of a parental responsibility agreement is the same as a court order conferring parental responsibility. Both may only be brought to an end by a court order on the application of a person with parental responsibility for the child or (with the leave of the court) of the child himself, if he has sufficient understanding to make the application [section 4(3) and (4)].

1.8. A court order which gives a father parental responsibility is similar to an order to give him parental rights and duties under section 4 of the Family Law Reform Act 1987. [An order under the 1987 Act which was in force at the commencement of the Children Act is deemed to be an order under section 4 of the latter statute: Schedule 14, paragraph 4]. Where a residence order is made in favour of a father [section 12(1)] an order under section 4 of the Children Act must be made. This is to ensure that a father who is entitled to have the child live with him under a court order will always have parental responsibility for him. If that residence order is later discharged, the parental responsibility order will not come to an end unless the court specifically decides that it should [section 12(4)]. A father who does not have parental responsibility is still a parent for the purpose of the Act.

Who Else may acquire Parental Responsibility?

1.9. People other than parents may acquire parental responsibility by appointment as a guardian or an order of the court (a residence order, a care order, or an emergency protection order).

Guardianship

1.10. A guardian may be appointed to take over parental responsibility for a child when a parent with parental responsibility dies. A guardian may be any other individual (including a parent). A local authority or voluntary organisation cannot be a guardian, since they are not 'individuals'. The guardian acquires parental responsibility (if he does not already have it) when the appointment takes effect [section 5(6)]. The guardian also acquires the right to agree (or to withhold agreement) to the child's adoption [Adoption Act 1976. section 16]. The Act clarifies the law of guardianship, enables appointments to be made more simply and introduces a number of new provisions which recognise that guardians are generally intended to take over the care of a child where he would not otherwise have a parent with parental responsibility.

1.11. Guardianship appointments may be made by a parent who has parental responsibility for the child or a person who has already been appointed guardian [section 5(3) and (4)]. An appointment must be in writing, dated and signed by (or at the direction of) the maker [section 5(5)]. If it is made at the appointer's direction, the making must be attested by two witnesses. An appointment may be made in a will or by deed, as under the old law, but does not have to be made in these ways.

1.12. Guardianship appointments will no longer always come into effect on the death of the maker. If, on the maker's death, the child still has a parent with parental responsibility, the appointment will not take effect until that parent also dies [section 5(7) and (8)]. The exception to this rule is that if, on the maker's death, there was a residence order in his favour, the appointment takes effect immediately (unless the residence order was also in favour of a surviving parent of the child)[section 5(7) and (9)]. Where a residence order was not in existence in favour of the appointer and a surviving parent, it is presumed that the surviving parent ought to be left to care for the child as he wishes. If he wants to seek the help or advice of the person named by the appointer, he may always do so. On the surviving parent's death, however, the appointed person becomes the guardian.

1.13. Guardianship appointments may be made individually or by people acting together [section 5(10)]. More than one guardian may be appointed by the same person or persons. A later appointment of a guardian (which is not clearly additional) will revoke an earlier one by the same person [section 6(1)]. A private appointment may also be revoked, either in writing which is dated and signed by the maker (or at his direction)[section 6(2)]. If the revocation is signed at the maker's direction, the signature must be in his presence and that of two witnesses who attest or by destruction of the appointment by the maker (or in his presence and at his direction) with the intention of revocation [section 6(3)]. An appointment made in a will or a codicil is revoked if the will or codicil is revoked [section 6(4)].

1.14. The guardian may disclaim his appointment in signed writing provided that he acts within a reasonable time of learning that the appointment has taken effect [section 6(5)]. Regulations may be made prescribing the manner of recording disclaimers [section 6(6)]. He may also be discharged by a court order made on the application of any person who has parental responsibility for the child, including the guardian himself, the child (if he has sufficient understanding) or by the court of its own initiative in any family proceedings [section 6(7)].

1.15. A court may appoint a guardian in similar circumstances to those in which a private appointment may take effect, namely:

(a) where a child has no parent with parental responsibility for him; or

(b) where, even though he still has such a parent, his other parent or a guardian of his has died and, immediately before his death, the deceased had a residence order in his favour in respect of the child [section 5(1)].

1.16 No court appointment may be made under section 5(5)(b) if the residence order in question was also in favour of a surviving parent of the child [section 5(9)]. Court appointments may be made on the application of the person who would like to be guardian or by the court of its own initiative in family proceedings [section 5(1) and (2)].

1.17. Guardians appointed by the court may be discharged in the same circumstances as private appointments.

Transitional Provisions

1.18. Where a guardian's appointment took effect before implementation of the Act. he is treated as if he had been appointed under the Act [Schedule 14, paragraph 12(1)]. He therefore acquires parental responsibility for the child concerned. However, any appointment which has not taken effect by that date will only have effect in accordance with the Act [Schedule 14, paragraph 13], so that the rules which limit the circumstances in which appointments have effect apply.

Residence Orders

1.19. A residence order may be made under Part II of the Act in order to settle the arrangements as to the person with whom a child is to live. *Where a residence order is made in favour of a person who is not a parent or guardian of the child it gives parental responsibility to him [Section 12(2)].*

1.20. A person who acquires parental responsibility under a residence order (i.e. someone who is not a parent or a guardian) does not acquire the right to agree or refuse to agree to the child's adoption (or other related adoption orders) or to appoint a guardian of the child [section 12(3)].

Care And Emergency Protection Orders

1.21 A residence order may not be made in favour of a local authority [section 9(2)]. However, a care order places a child in the care of a local authority, which enables them to decide with whom the child will live, and also gives them parental responsibility [section 33(1) and (3)(a)]. It does not give them the right to agree or refuse to agree to adoption or to appoint a guardian [section 33(6)(b)] but the local authority may apply to the court to have the appointment discharged. It also does not enable them to cause the child to be brought up in a religious persuasion other than the one in which he would have been brought up if the order had not been made [section 33(6)(a)].

1.22. Emergency protection orders are short term orders which entitle the applicant to remove the child from (or to prevent him from being removed to) a situation of apprehended danger. These orders confer parental responsibility on the applicant for the period of the order [section 44(4)(c)]. A person with parental responsibility under an emergency protection order must take (but may only take) action which is reasonably required to safeguard or promote the child's welfare (bearing in mind the duration of the order)[section 44(5)(b)].

Effect of Existing Orders

1.23 A person who otherwise would not have parental responsibility for the child but who had care and control or custody of a child under an existing order is given parental responsibility while that order lasts [Schedule 14 paragraph 7(1)]. Such a person (for example a 'custodian' under the Children Act 1975) is also treated in specific instances as if he had the benefit of a residence order. He may apply for a section 8 order without leave, for example. and, if he had care and control of the child (rather than custody without care and control), certain other provisions apply: [Schedule 14, paragraphs 7 and 8]. Thus, a father who does not have parental responsibility for his child because he is not married to the child's mother, but who had care and control or custody under an existing order, is deemed to have a 'parental responsibility order' in his favour [Schedule 14, paragraph 6]. A person with an access order under the old law is not given parental responsibility but is treated for certain purposes in the Act as if he had a contact order [Schedule 14, paragraph 9]. In exceptional circumstances, he may be required to disobey an order which would otherwise put the child at risk. [Pursuant to the duty not to cause unnecessary suffering in section 1 of the Children and Young Persons Act 1933].

The Exercise Of Parental Responsibility

1.24. The fact that one person acquires parental responsibility does not in itself remove another's parental responsibility [section 2(6)]. *After separation or divorce parents retain their parental responsibility.* However, a person who has parental responsibility is not entitled to act incompatibly with a court order [section 2(8)]. Existing orders regarding custody, legal custody, care and control and access continue to have effect after the Act comes into force. The fact that a person has parental responsibility for a child under the Act does not mean that he may act incompatibly with an existing order [Schedule 14, paragraphs 6(3) and 7(3)].

1.25. Parental responsibility for a child cannot be passed on to someone else or otherwise be given up [section 2(9)]. However, where a person acquired parental responsibility under a court order (or parental responsibility agreement or by appointment as guardian). the court may later bring that order (or agreement or appointment) to an end.

1.26. A person with parental responsibility may arrange for another person to meet that responsibility on his behalf [section 2(9)]. Such an arrangement might be useful while a person with parental responsibility is unable to act, perhaps due to a stay in hospital or a trip abroad. It does not affect any liability of the person with parental responsibility which follows from a failure to meet his parental responsibility [section 2(11)].

1.27. Where more than one person has parental responsibility for a child at the same time, one may act independently of the other or others to meet that responsibility [section 2(5) and (7)]. The Act does *not* repeat the old law in its attempts to impose a duty on one parent to consult the other or to give one a right of veto against the action of the other. If necessary, one person with parental responsibility may ask a court to make a specific issue order or condition in a residence order which would require the other to inform him before a particular step is taken or not taken [section 8 and 11(7)(b)]. The onus of applying to court will not generally fall on the person who is caring for the child. This person will therefore be able to respond to circumstances as they arise.

When A Child is in Care

1.28. The only exception to the rule which permits independent action to meet shared parental responsibility arises when a child is in care. Here, the local authority is given power to determine the extent to which another person with parental responsibility may act. [section 33(3)(b) and (4)].

Care But Not Parental Responsibility

1.29. If a person has care of a child for whom he does not have parental responsibility, section 3(5) of the Act empowers him to do what is reasonable in all the circumstances to safeguard or promote the child's welfare. This is the person who in old terminology had 'actual custody' of the child. Of course, such a person may not act in a way which conflicts with the Act, in particular with an order under it, except in the limited circumstances in which he may be required to protect the child from danger.

Private Proceedings

1.30. In the area of private law the Act seeks to strike a balance between the need to recognise the child as an independent person and to ensure that his views are fully taken into account, and the risk of casting on him the burden of resolving problems caused by his parents or requiring him to choose between them. As well as including his views in the checklist, the Act allows a child with sufficient understanding to seek an order about his own future [section 10(8)]. The court rules enable the child to be joined as a party if the court thinks fit even if he does not seek an order.

1.31. Whether or not the child is a party to proceedings, the court has the power to commission a welfare report and to ensure that it covers his wishes and feelings [section 7].

1.32. In private law proceedings between parents or other individuals, the orders available under the Act look to practicalities. Thus the courts have the power to make orders about:

- with whom the child will live (residence orders);
- any form of contact he is to have with other people (contact orders);
- any other particular matter concerning the child and upbringing (specific issue orders), or,
- to prohibit anything being done in relation to the child (prohibited steps orders).

1.33. Unlike custody orders, court orders do not remove parental power and authority from one parent or confer sole power and authority on the other. Rather they settle particular matters which neither party may then upset. Parents will still be able to act as parents in ways which are not affected by the order. The orders themselves are much more flexible, allowing the court to make whatever arrangements seem best in the particular case. Wardship remains available to private individuals but the breadth of new orders should make the need to use it rarer.

Family Assistance Orders

1.34. A family assistance order may only last for up to six months [section 16(5)] and is designed to give expert help to families. It will be particularly useful where there has been separation or divorce and a family needs assistance to cope with problems arising during what may be a difficult period of transition. In part this new order replaces the supervision order which could be made under the old law in divorce and other family proceedings. Unlike those supervision orders, family assistance orders may be made even if the court makes no other order in respect of the child. They may be used to promote co-operation within the family so that, for example, arrangements for contact with the child may be established, even if no contact order has been made. If a section 8 order has been made with respect to the child and the officer providing the assistance thinks that it should be varied or discharged, he may bring the case before the court [section 16(6)].

1.35. A court may make a family assistance order in family proceedings where it has power to make an order under Part II of the Act and there are exceptional circumstances [section 16(1) and (3)(a)]. Under a family assistance order a local authority or probation officer will be made available to give advice and assistance to (and, where appropriate, befriend) a person named in the order [section 16(1)]. The person or persons named in the order may be the child himself, a parent or guardian of his or any person with whom the child lives or in whose favour a contact order is in force with respect to the child [section 16(2)]. Before an order may be made each person named in it (except the child) must have given his consent [section 16(3)(b)].

1.36. Most family assistance orders will probably appoint a probation officer to carry them out. Probation officers (acting as divorce court welfare officers) will usually have had involvement with the family when compiling a welfare report. However, where a local authority has worked with the family or has compiled the report, one of their officers might be a more appropriate appointment. The order may require a person named in it to assist the officer involved by informing him of the address of named persons and allowing him to visit them [section 16(4)]. A further family assistance order may be sought in appropriate cases.

Private Law Orders

1.37. The court may use private law orders to safeguard the welfare of children as well as to resolve disputes between parents. For example a residence order may be made in favour of a person willing to care for a child, perhaps a relative, so that the child need not be made subject to a care order or remain in local authority accommodation. Anyone who has or can show a proper interest in the child may apply for any section 8 order. To protect against these orders being used improperly to interfere in families, those who can apply for an order are generally limited to parents and others who have some legal responsibility for the child or who have cared for him for a substantial period. But other people will be able to apply if they get the court's permission (although there are special rules about local authority foster parents, who are in a rather different position from members of the child's family) [sections 9 and 10].

Referral to the Local Authority

1.38. A court which is hearing family proceedings in which a question arises about the welfare of a child may direct a local authority to investigate the child's circumstances if it appears that a care or supervision order may be appropriate [section 37(1)].

1.39. A direction requires the local authority to consider whether to take any action with respect to the child, such as applying for a care or supervision order or providing services or assistance to the child or his family [section 37(2)]. If the authority decide not to apply for a care or supervision order they must report their decision to the court, giving their reasons and details of any action (including the provision of services or assistance) they are taking or propose to take with respect to the child [section 37(3)]. This information must be provided within eight weeks of the direction, unless the court otherwise directs [section 37(4)]. They must also consider whether the child's circumstances should be reviewed and, if so, decide when that review should begin [section 37(6)].

1.40. This power to direct a local authority investigation replaces the court's power to make a care or supervision order of their own motion 'in exceptional circumstances'. Under the Act a care or supervision order may only be made when the local authority or an authorised person has applied for either such order. Care and supervision orders place such important responsibilities on local authorities that it is left to them to decide, taking into account the circumstances identified in their investigation, whether or not to apply for an order. Moreover, it will be for them to decide what services may be provided to the family which might remove the need for a court order. However, the court may make an interim care or supervision order pending the outcome of the investigation [section 38(1)(b)].

EXAMPLES OF COMMITTEE STRUCTURE, OFFICER SUPPORT AND ADVISORY GROUPS

Committee Structure

1. A joint sub-committee of the Social Services and Education Committees may be set up. Membership of the sub-committee may be drawn from both committees and members from, for example, committees responsible for housing and leisure services and could include co- opted people to represent health authority, voluntary sector, private childcare sector and employer interests. The sub-committee could report to the Social Services and Education Committees. It would have delegated powers to act on behalf of both Committees under the terms of reference concerning the matters referred to it. These would be general service provisions and could include policy in relation to services for under eights, joint planning and monitoring of services.

2. Social Services and Education Committees may agree to set up jointly an under eights sub-committee to undertake tasks of a general service nature such as joint planning and monitoring of services. The sub-committee would have delegated authority to act under the terms of reference of the Social Services Committee and the Education Committee.

Officer Support

3. The legislation on education and social services functions requires there to be posts of Chief Education Officer and Director of Social Services. There are no other statutory posts and local authorities are free to make whatever arrangements they think appropriate to enable staff in social services and education departments to work together. There is no legal barrier to setting up an under eights department staffed by officers with qualifications and/or experience in day care or nursery education and giving it day to day responsibility for services for under eights including planning (where appropriate) implementation and monitoring within the general policies agreed by either the Social Services or the Education Committee or jointly.

6. The local authority may fund a post with a remit to work on co-ordination of services, organisation of training and support for under eights committees and local liaison groups. Local authorities which decide to create such posts may place responsibility for managing the person appointed within social services or education or the two departments jointly.

Advisory Groups

7. Local authorities may set up an advisory group with representation from social services and education, recreation, housing, health authorities, voluntary bodies, private providers, employers and trades unions. These groups could advise the Social Services and Education Committees on issues relating to under eights.

8. Voluntary organisations in a local authority area may, probably with encouragement and help from the local authority, set up a forum to ensure that their representatives on a committee or advisory group are able to represent their interests fully.

9. Area or local liaison/co-ordination groups may be set up to cover a part of a local authority area. These involve all the early years workers in the locality including people in the voluntary sector.

TYPES OF DAY CARE SERVICES USED BY UNDER FIVES AND SCHOOL AGE CHILDREN AND EDUCATIONAL SERVICES FOR THE UNDER FIVES

Day Nurseries

Day nurseries look after under fives for the length of the adult working day. They may be run by social services departments, voluntary organisations, private companies or individuals as a business, community groups as a co-operative enterprise, employers in the public or private sectors including local authorities and health authorities and Government Departments for their workforce, or any of these bodies on a partnership basis. Children will attend part-time or full-time depending on their and their parents' needs.

Playgroups

Playgroups provide sessional care for children aged between three and five. though some may take children at 2½. They aim to provide learning experiences through structured play opportunities in groups, and with involvement of the parents in all aspects of the operation of the group. Most playgroups are run on a self-help basis by groups of parents with one or two paid staff. A few are run by local authorities. Some are called opportunity groups and cater specifically for children with special needs. Playgroup sessions last for no longer than 4 hours.

Extended day playgroups

These provide care for children for more than 4 hours a day and many will be used by working parents on the same basis as a day nursery.

Creches

This term is commonly used to describe two different facilities: a day nursery managed by or on behalf of an employer for the children of his employees; or a facility attached to a shopping centre or shop or leisure centre where children are left by their parents for short spells of time. Both types are like day nurseries.

Private Nursery Schools

These institutions vary considerably in character but all offer educational and day care facilities. They will be open for the length of the school day during term time.

Nursery Units of Independent Schools

These are integral parts of an independent school and provide for early access to the school. Children usually attend part-time.

Maintained Nursery Schools and Classes

Nursery schools are establishments with their own legal identity. Nursery classes or units are integral parts of primary schools. Both kinds of provision are open during the normal school day but the great majority of children attend part-time, commonly five mornings or five afternoons a week.

Reception Classes in Primary Schools

A large number of primary schools admit children to reception classes before they are five. Most are four-year-olds admitted at the start of the school year or the term in which they reach five. The great majority attend full-time.

Combined Nursery Centres

These centres combine educational and day care facilities and are managed jointly by education and social services departments. They take children from 18 months to the age of five, and some who are younger. They may offer a range of support services to parents.

Childminders

Childminders look after children aged under five and school age children outside school hours and in the holidays in domestic premises, usually the childminder's own home. They offer this service all the year round for the full adult working day. Parents and childminders negotiate the terms and conditions.

Carers in the child's home

Some parents employ a nanny or mother's help or au pair to look after the child or children in the home. This is a private arrangement, like childminding, with both parties agreeing about terms and conditions.

Out Of School Clubs

These offer to care for the school age child in the absence of the parents or carers from the end of the school day until the parent can collect the child and also sometimes before school starts. They are not open access. They may be run by the local authority, voluntary or community group or private company. Children will be escorted to the club by a responsible person and not allowed to leave until collected by the parent or person who has parental responsibility or who is looking after the child.

Holiday Schemes

These look after children of school age during the school holidays and operate like out of school clubs.

Supervised Activities

This term covers specific activities provided for school age children out of school hours and in the holidays. They will not purport to care for the child because the parents are not available. Leisure centres may offer supervised activities for children who will be instructed in a particular skill or sport or pastime. The arrangements for bringing and collecting the children will vary and there may or may not be a limit on numbers.

Adventure Playgrounds

These provide open access play facilities for children of all ages, but they are normally attended by children of school age. They will have some fixed equipment and there will be some supervision. Some voluntary groups have developed adventure playgrounds specially for children with disabilities. Most will place no limit on numbers and will not require formal arrangements for bringing and collecting the children. They will be open all day in the holidays and at half term.

Other Play Opportunities

These include play sessions in playgrounds, local parks or community centres. Some libraries organise play sessions on an irregular basis and voluntary bodies or community or special interest groups will put on organised events during the school holidays. District Councils, Police Departments and other bodies also organise activities for school age children. Many will be open access, but some will place a limit on numbers.

NOTES ON PLANNING, FIRE SAFETY, FOOD HYGIENE AND HEALTH AND SAFETY

SECTION A   PLANNING PROCEDURES

Legislation

1. Primary legislation is the Town and Country Planning Act 1990. Section 55 defines 'development' where a planning application must be made as 'the carrying out of building, engineering, mining, or other operations in, on, over or under land, or the making of any material change in the use of any buildings or other land'.

Subordinate legislation is in the Town and Country Planning (Use Classes) Order 1987. This groups into classes those uses of land which, from the planning point of view, have similar implications for local amenity. The effect is to exclude from the definition of development, and hence from planning control, changes of use where the existing and proposed uses fall into the same class.

Planning Requirements

2. Where construction of new buildings or a material change of use of an existing building is involved, a planning application to the local planning authority (Metropolitan District or London Borough or District Council in a shire county) is required. It should be noted that there are two situations where proposals in some cases may not have to be made the subject of a planning application.

(a) *Domestic Premises*
Planning permission may not be needed for day care facilities on a modest scale on existing residential property (ie providing the character and use of the building remain essentially residential). Internal alterations or installation of toilet or washroom facilities do not need planning permission.

(b) *Non-Domestic Premises*
The planning system is concerned with the primary use of buildings or land. Ancillary uses are not subject to planning control. Many employers may in this way be able to set aside part of their premises for a day nursery for the children of their employees without having to make a planning application.

The provisions in **The Use Classes Order** give some flexibility. Where buildings listed below are used for the following purposes, changing their use to a day nursery or other day care service, is not material and therefore planning permission is not required:

i.   Provision of any medical or health service other than premises attached to the residence of the consultant or practitioner;

ii.   a day centre;

iii.   provision of education;

iv.   for sale of works of art;

v.   as a museum;

vi.   as a public library or reading room;

vii.   as a public or exhibition hall;

viii. for or in connection with public worship or religious instruction.

Formal Determination of Need for Planning Permission

3. It is possible to obtain a formal determination of the need for planning permission by applying to the local planning authority for a ruling (a section 64 Determination). No forms are needed and no fee is payable. The planning authority should be written to and given a description of the proposed

development and its location. A determination can only be given if development has not already begun.

Leaflets

4. The following are considered useful:

Appendix II to Assessing the Case and Setting up a Nursery: A Managers Guide (Office of the Minister for the Civil Service – OMCS);

A Step by Step Guide to Planning Permission for Small Businesses (free from local planning authorities).

SECTION B   FIRE SAFETY REQUIREMENTS

Legislation

1. The two main Acts on fire safety are:

- The Fire Services Act 1947;
- The Fire Precautions Act 1971 as amended by the Fire Safety and Safety of Places of Sport Act 1987.

2. The Fire Services Act 1947 requires fire authorities to give advice on fire safety when requested. This advice is available free of charge to any person or regulatory authority who requests it. Fire officers will inspect premises at the request of social services departments to advise on their suitability for the purposes of childminding or day care. Social services departments should encourage day care providers and childminders to approach their local fire brigade for advice on fire safety.

3. The Fire Precautions Act 1971 covers fire precautions in occupied premises and is administered by fire authorities. Under this Act certain premises require a fire certificate, which will specify fire precautions such as:

- the means of escape;
- fire fighting equipment;
- means of warning in the event of fire etc.

The fire brigade has to ensure that any statutory requirements made under the Fire Precautions Act are complied with.

4. The Fire Precautions Act does not apply to single private dwellings. In such domestic premises (or other premises not requiring a fire certificate) fire authorities will advise on whether fire safety standards are adequate for the planned use.

Training for Day Care Providers

5. It is a general requirement attached to fire certificates that all people who work in buildings for which a fire certificate is required shall be given instruction and training to ensure that they understand the fire precautions and action to be taken in the event of fire. The training should include people on regular duties or shift duties working outside normal working hours, including part- time staff, cleaners etc. These arrangements must take account of the special needs of anyone likely to be on the premises, for example anyone with a physical handicap.

6. In non-certificated premises much depends on the fire safety awareness and initiative of local management. Sensible fire precautions and good housekeeping practices will reduce the possibility of having a fire and needing to evacuate the building. All staff should receive instruction on how to raise the alarm if they discover a fire, on the action to take on being alerted to a fire and in the practical use of the portable fire fighting equipment provided.

7. The local fire brigade may be contacted for specific advice. Many brigades are also able to provide suitable locally produced fire safety literature.

8. Particular care is needed over:

- means of escape;
- heating and fire guards;
- electrical safety;
- storage of flammable materials.

General Fire Safety

9. A smoke alarm should be fitted in domestic premises used for childminding.

10. A child should not be able to gain unsupervised access to a kitchen.

SECTION C   FOOD HYGIENE

Main Legislation

The Food Safety Act 1990

1. This Act replaced much of the Food Act 1984 and widened the range of powers of Enforcement Officers. These new powers include the right to issue Improvement Notices and Emergency Prohibition Notices.

2. Improvement Notices, for example, may be served where the Enforcement Officer has reasonable grounds for believing that the proprietor of a food business is not complying with, say, a requirement of the Food Hygiene (General) Regulations 1970 [as amended].

The Food Hygiene (General) Regulations 1970

3. These Regulations apply to any business in which any person engages in the handling of food.

In the main, the requirements cover:

(a) the prohibition of carrying on a food business in any premises which is insanitary or its condition is such that food is exposed to the risk of contamination;

(b) the cleanliness of articles and equipment which are likely to come into contact with food;

(c) protecting food from the risk of contamination;

(d) the personal cleanliness of food handlers, including their clothing and the action to be taken if they suffer from or are carriers of infections likely to cause food borne diseases;

(e) the construction of the food premises. including the requirements for a wholesome water supply, suitable washing up facilities, handbasins, lighting, ventilation, sanitary conveniences and accommodation for clothing;

(f) the cleanliness and repair of food rooms and the prevention of any risk of infestation by pests;

(g) the proper disposal of waste material.

The Food Hygiene (Amendment) Regulations 1990

4. These Regulations introduce temperature controls for certain foods, require that relevant foods be kept below 8°C or above 63°C and from 1 April 1993, require some foods to be kept below 5°C.

5. The enforcing authority for the above legislation is the local authority Environmental Health Officer who can give advice.

Training

6. Although the local Environmental Health Officer is an invaluable source of advice, this Officer is invariably only at an establishment for a relatively short time and consequently not all conditions and practices on which advice may be given would be apparent to the Officer. The need to produce safe food of good quality rests with the establishment. It is therefore prudent for all food handlers to be trained in basic food hygiene – the Government is considering making it a legal requirement for food handlers to be so trained. The local Environmental Health Officer may be able to provide this service or give advice on where such training may be obtained.

Further Information

7. Further information may be obtained from:

(a) HSC HYGIENE, 2nd Edition, HMSO, 1988, ISBN 0-11-321095-7 (to be republished).

(b) FOOD HANDLERS GUIDE – CLEAN FOOD, 2nd Edition, HMSO, 1990, ISBN 0-11-321264X.

(c) THE GUIDELINES ON THE FOOD HYGIENE (AMENDMENT) REGULATIONS, HMSO, 1990, ISBN 0-11-321369-7.

(d) YOUR GUIDE TO THE FOOD HYGIENE (GENERAL) REGULATIONS, 1970 free from Department of Health, Room 604, Eileen House, Newington Causeway, London, SE1 6EF.

SECTION D   HEALTH AND SAFETY REQUIREMENTS FOR DAY CARE PROVIDERS

Legislation

The Health and Safety at Work etc Act 1974

1. This Act lays down the essential health and safety responsibilities for employers, employees and the self-employed. Its main aim is to secure the health, safety and welfare of persons at work and to protect third parties against risks to their health and safety arising from the work activities of others. The following are statutory regulations made under the Act:

(a) **The Electricity at Work Regulations 1989**

These regulations require all electrical equipment and systems to be safe to use, properly installed and maintained and worked on by competent persons.

(b) **The Reporting of Injuries, Diseases and Dangerous Occurrences Regulations 1985**

All fatal and major injuries which occur to any person as a result of work activity must be reported to the enforcing authority (either the Health and Safety Executive or the Local Authority, depending on the type of work activity). Similarly all injuries to employees which result in their being off work for more than three days must be reported as above. Certain diseases and dangerous occurrences must also be reported.

(c) **The Health and Safety (Information for Employees) Regulations 1989**

Every employer is required to display an official poster or provide leaflets for employees which set out basic information on health and safety law in an easily understandable form.

Health and Safety Requirements

Domestic Premises

2. The Health and Safety at Work Act does not apply to 'domestic premises'. Therefore it is not relevant in the case of childminders applying for registration.

Non-domestic Premises

3. Persons in charge of non-domestic premises, which they make available for use by those not in their employment, have duties to take such steps as are reasonable to ensure that there are no risks to health and safety. These duties extend to the premises themselves, any connected premises, such as corridors. stairs and storage premises, the ways into and out of the premises and any machinery, equipment and substances in the premises (section 4, Health and Safety at Work Act.).

Duties of Employers

4. Employers have general duties towards their employees and others, not in their employment, who might be affected by their activities. These are broadly expressed as being to ensure that:

i. equipment is safe and without risk to health;

ii. premises are safe and properly maintained and the working environment is safe and healthy;

iii. adequate information, training and supervision is given to ensure health and safety;

iv. any materials are properly handled, stored and carried so as to prevent risk.

Training

5. Training in health and safety matters should be sufficient to ensure that employees know how to ensure their own safety and that of any children they are caring for. The same standards are expected of the self-employed.

Further Information

6. Further information is available from any Health and Safety Executive office from whom the following leaflets are available:

> Health and Safety at Work etc Act:
> The Act Outlined (HSC2)
> Advice to Employees (HSC5)
> Reporting an Injury or Dangerous Occurrence (HSCII Rev)
> Guidance for Small Businesses on Electricity at Work (IND(G)89(1))

A Guide to the Health and Safety at Work etc Act 1974 (LI). from HMSO and Government Bookshops gives more detailed information.

Printed in the United Kingdom for HMSO
Dd 295157 C75 11/91